Grammar Practice Book

Scott Foresman

Editorial Offices: Glenview, Illinois • Parsippany, New Jersey • New York, New York
Sales Offices: Reading, Massachusetts • Duluth, Georgia • Glenview, Illinois
Carrollton, Texas • Ontario, California

Editorial Offices
Glenview, Illinois • Parsippany, New Jersey • New York, New York

Sales Offices
Reading, Massachusetts • Duluth, Georgia • Glenview, Illinois
Carrollton, Texas • Ontario, California

ISBN 0-328-00669-6

6 7 8 9 10-DBH-06 05 04 03 02 01

Table of Contents

Unit 1 **Sentences**

Unit 2 **Nouns**

Unit 3 Verbs

Goals Great and Small

Unit 4 Adjectives and Adverbs

Unit 5 Pronouns, Prepositions, Conjunctions, and Interjections

Into the Unknown

Unit 6 Sentence Parts and Punctuating Sentences

Name ______________________________

REVIEW

Sentences

Directions: Read each group of words. Write **S** if it is a sentence. Write **NS** if it is not a sentence.

______________ **1.** During my summer vacation, I visited the United Nations for the first time.

______________ **2.** Located in New York City.

______________ **3.** It began with 50 member countries.

______________ **4.** Now has a total of 185 member countries.

______________ **5.** The UN has its own flag and stamps!

______________ **6.** Even a web site of its own!

______________ **7.** I was very impressed by the building.

______________ **8.** All the flags from all the nations.

______________ **9.** People from many countries, many in colorful native clothing.

______________ **10.** I really enjoy learning new things.

Directions: Add a word or group of words to complete each sentence. Write the complete sentence on the line. Remember to start each sentence with a capital letter.

11. For the first time, I _____.

____

12. _____ was very exciting!

____

13. I could hardly wait to _____.

____

14. _____ was the best experience of all!

____

15. I recommend _____.

____

Notes for Home: Your child identified and wrote complete sentences. ***Home Activity:*** Together, write a letter or postcard to a family member or friend. Use complete sentences.

Name ______________________________

Kinds of Sentences—Declarative, Interrogative, Imperative, and Exclamatory

There are four kinds of sentences. Each begins with a capital letter and ends with a special end mark.

A **declarative sentence** makes a statement. It ends with a period.

The rudder on any boat is a steering device.

An **interrogative sentence** asks a question. It ends with a question mark.

Doesn't an airplane have a rudder too?

An **imperative sentence** gives a command or makes a request. It ends with a period. The subject *(you)* is not shown, but it is understood.

Fasten your life jacket, please.

An **exclamatory sentence** expresses strong feeling. It ends with an exclamation mark.

So many facts about boats are new to me!

Directions: Write whether each sentence is **declarative, interrogative, imperative,** or **exclamatory.**

______________________ **1.** I'm planning to take up sailing.

______________________ **2.** What fun it would be to sail the ocean blue!

______________________ **3.** Are there still pirates lurking around the ocean?

______________________ **4.** Read this true story about piracy.

______________________ **5.** I have a dream of sailing around the world.

Directions: Write the correct end punctuation to complete each sentence.

6. Sailing lessons can be confusing _____

7. You have to understand about wind, currents, and angles _____

8. Try not to become discouraged _____

9. Did you know that even famous navigators had some troubles _____

10. Focus on one thing at a time _____

Notes for Home: Your child identified four kinds of sentences and added end punctuation to sentences. ***Home Activity:*** Read with your child and work together to identify different kinds of sentences. Ask your child to tell you about different end punctuation marks.

Kinds of Sentences—Declarative, Interrogative, Imperative, and Exclamatory

Directions: Add the correct end punctuation to each sentence.

1. Tami was sure she was braver than anyone else _____
2. Isn't she afraid of anything _____
3. She should be careful around strange animals _____
4. What a narrow escape I had yesterday _____
5. I mistakenly thought a wild animal was tame _____
6. Climb the cliff with us _____
7. Don't forget the mountain climbers' rules _____
8. I was absolutely terrified _____
9. Some people are afraid of heights _____
10. Aren't you ever afraid _____

Directions: Read each sentence and decide which kind of sentence it is. Then change it to the kind of sentence named in ( ). Write the new sentence on the line, using correct end punctuation.

11. Do we believe in using common sense? (declarative)

____

12. You can ask the Appalachian Mountain Club for advice. (imperative)

____

13. Think about climbing Mount Everest. (interrogative)

____

14. Would that be a wonderful adventure? (exclamatory)

____

15. You haven't ever climbed Mount Washington. (interrogative)

____

Write a Paragraph

On a separate sheet of paper, write a paragraph about an event you remember. Use at least one of each of the four kinds of sentences in your paragraph.

Notes for Home: Your child identified and wrote different kinds of sentences. ***Home Activity:*** Say different kinds of sentences aloud. Have your child use hand signs to show the end punctuation for each one. For example, point a forefinger for a period.

Name ______________________

RETEACHING

Kinds of Sentences— Declarative, Interrogative, Imperative, and Exclamatory

Read the directions below. Write your responses in complete sentences.

1. Make a statement that tells what is pictured. Use a period at the end of your sentence.

 ____

2. Tell exactly how you feel about the spider. Express yourself strongly with an exclamation mark.

 ____

3. Give the spider a command. Use a period.

 ____

4. Ask the spider why it did not obey you. Use a question mark.

 ____

A **declarative sentence** makes a statement. An **interrogative sentence** asks a question. An **imperative sentence** gives a command or makes a request. An **exclamatory sentence** expresses strong feeling.

Directions: Write **declarative, interrogative, exclamatory,** or **imperative** to describe each sentence.

______________ **1.** Tell me about your nature walk.

______________ **2.** Did you see the bright orange salamander?

______________ **3.** What a beautiful beetle that is!

______________ **4.** Are earthworms good for the soil?

______________ **5.** Ants are very strong for their size.

______________ **6.** Listen for the crickets on summer evenings.

______________ **7.** How slowly those snails move!

______________ **8.** Lightning bugs glow in the dark.

Notes for Home: Your child identified declarative, interrogative, imperative, and exclamatory sentences. ***Home Activity:*** Have your child look at advertisements in newspapers and magazines and identify each type of sentence he or she finds.

Name ____

Kinds of Sentences—Declarative, Interrogative, Imperative, and Exclamatory

Directions: Add end punctuation. Circle any letters that need capitalization.

1. how interesting the solar system is ________
2. venus is covered with thick clouds ________
3. Jupiter, the largest planet, has the shortest day ________
4. which planet would you visit first ________
5. Look through a telescope at the craters on the moon ________
6. Did you know that Mercury is closest to the sun ________
7. what a great distance Pluto is from the sun ________
8. Watch for meteor showers in June, August, and December ________
9. the polar caps on Mars change with the seasons ________
10. What are the lines on the surface of Mars ________
11. How vast the Milky Way is ________
12. it has more than 100 billion stars ________

Directions: Use the sentence below to write new sentences about Saturn. Write the kind of sentence asked for in ( ).

Saturn is a bright planet with beautiful rings.

13. ____ (interrogative)
14. ____ (exclamatory)
15. ____ (imperative)
16. ____ (declarative)
17. ____ (imperative)

Write a Letter

On a separate sheet of paper, write a letter to the President. Tell why you should be one of the first students chosen to take a trip to the moon. Explain your motivations, and ask questions about space. Add variety to your writing by using different kinds of sentences.

Notes for Home: Your child punctuated and wrote four types of sentences. ***Home Activity:*** Write a declarative sentence. (For example: *We walked out the door.*) Together, change the sentence into an imperative sentence, an interrogative sentence, and an exclamatory sentence.

Name ______________________________ Teammates

Four Kinds of Sentences

REVIEW

Directions: Add the correct punctuation mark to the end of each sentence. Then tell whether the sentence is **declarative, interrogative, imperative,** or **exclamatory.**

______________ **1.** Intolerance usually results from a lack of information _____

______________ **2.** Do you feel uncomfortable, for example, around a person with a disability _____

______________ **3.** Don't let this feeling make you ignore the person _____

______________ **4.** A good friend may be right in front of you _____

______________ **5.** Make the effort to find out more about this person _____

Directions: Write five sentences about someone who has experienced prejudice from others. It can be a real person or an imaginary character. Write the kind of sentence shown in ( ). Remember to start each sentence with a capital letter and end each one with the correct end punctuation.

6. (declarative)

____

____

7. (interrogative)

____

____

8. (declarative)

____

____

9. (imperative)

____

____

10. (exclamatory)

____

____

Notes for Home: Your child identified and wrote the four different kinds of sentences and added the correct punctuation mark at the end of each of them. ***Home Activity:*** Challenge your child to use the same word—such as *dog* or *school*—in each of the four kinds of sentences.

Name ______________________________ **Teammates**

Subjects and Predicates

The **subject** is the word or group of words about which something is said in the sentence. All the words in the subject are called the **complete subject.** The most important word in the complete subject is called the **simple subject.** It is usually a noun or a pronoun. Some simple subjects, such as *Jackie Robinson,* are more than one word.

All citizens can enjoy one another's talents and ideas.

The **predicate** is the word or group of words that tells something about the subject. All the words in the predicate make up the **complete predicate.** The most important word in the complete predicate is the verb. It is called the **simple predicate.** Some simple predicates can have more than one word.

People from other countries may bring us new music and foods.

A sentence fragment is a group of words that looks like a sentence but does not express a complete thought. Correct sentence fragments by adding words to make a complete sentence or by joining the fragment to a related sentence.

Sentence fragment: The names of immigrants' music and foods.

Sentence: The names of immigrants' music and foods add words to American English.

Directions: Decide if the underlined group of words is the complete subject, the complete predicate, or a sentence fragment. Circle **CS, CP,** or **SF** to show your answer.

1.	The five girls enjoyed the overnight trip.	CS	CP	SF
2.	The clear blue lake was beautiful.	CS	CP	SF
3.	Set up their tents at night.	CS	CP	SF
4.	Millions of stars sparkled overhead.	CS	CP	SF
5.	Each girl had brought some homemade food.	CS	CP	SF
6.	Alanna O'Brien offered Irish bread.	CS	CP	SF
7.	The happy girls ate Denise's Greek baklava for dessert.	CS	CP	SF
8.	The girls in the group.	CS	CP	SF
9.	They packed up their tents.	CS	CP	SF
10.	Climbed into their van again.	CS	CP	SF

Notes for Home: Your child has learned to identify complete subjects, complete predicates, and sentence fragments. ***Home Activity:*** Play a game in which you or your child gives a complete subject and the other person adds a complete predicate to form a complete sentence.

Subjects and Predicates

Directions: For each sentence, underline the complete subject once. Underline the complete predicate twice. Then circle the simple subject and simple predicate.

1. Banneker Middle School had a fine glee club.
2. It was holding auditions last week.
3. Dominic wanted to join that musical group.
4. Mr. Dixon, the glee club director, gave him a voice test.
5. The boy was singing way off key.
6. Some students in the glee club were snickering.
7. Their unkind behavior displeased the director.
8. However, Dominic simply shrugged his shoulders.
9. He said something to Mr. Dixon.
10. The surprised director waved a hand toward the piano.

Directions: Correct each sentence fragment by adding words to make it a complete sentence. Write the new sentence on the line.

11. Some sheet music.

____

12. Could read the music and was playing it!

____

13. The singers in the glee club.

____

14. Asked Dominic to be the glee club pianist.

____

15. At glee club practice after that.

____

Write an Invitation

On a separate sheet of paper, write an invitation to a friend to go to a concert with you. Use complete sentences. Identify the simple subject and predicate in each.

Notes for Home: Your child identified simple and complete subjects and predicates in sentences and corrected sentence fragments. ***Home Activity:*** Ask your child to explain these terms, using the exercises above as examples.

Name ________________________________

RETEACHING

Subjects and Predicates

In each of the complete sentences, underline the complete subject once and the complete predicate twice. Circle the simple subject and the simple predicate. Put a check by the sentence fragment.

1. Six members of the team looked for a good place to watch the animals.
2. Plenty of sunlight to see the lions.
3. We all worked together to reach our common goal.

The **subject** is the word or group of words about which something is said in a sentence. The most important part of the subject is called the **simple subject.** It is usually a noun or a pronoun. All the words in the subject make up the **complete subject.** The **predicate** is the word or group of words that tells something about the subject. The most important part of the predicate is the verb. It is called the **simple predicate.** All the words in the predicate make up the **complete predicate.** A **sentence fragment** is an incomplete sentence.

Directions: Draw a line through each sentence fragment. In each complete sentence, underline the complete subject once. Circle the simple subject. Then underline the complete predicate twice and circle the simple predicate.

1. Some lions live in the wild.
2. Most male lions are larger than female lions.
3. Cubs are young lions.
4. Live together in a group called a pride.
5. A group of lions may include over ten animals.
6. The diet of lions is mostly meat.
7. Sleep many more hours per day than humans do.
8. All wild lions hunt other animals.
9. Children of many countries.
10. Special people train lions for the circus.
11. The fascinated crowds admire the beauty and strength of lions.
12. Some wild animals live freely in Africa and Asia.
13. The powerful lion is known as "the king of beasts."
14. Of a lion in a zoo is twenty to twenty-five years.

Notes for Home: Your child identified sentence fragments and simple subjects and predicates. ***Home Activity:*** Together, read a movie review. Then read the subject of one sentence. Have your child write a new predicate. Read a predicate and have your child write a subject.

Name ______________________________

Subjects and Predicates

Directions: Draw a line between the complete subject and the complete predicate in each sentence. Circle each simple subject and simple predicate.

1. Several cities served as the capital before 1800.
2. The national government moved away from Philadelphia.
3. Washington, D.C. has been the capital since then.
4. George Washington chose a location in 1791.
5. His choice included land in both Maryland and Virginia.
6. Those states gave their land to the government.
7. Congress located the capital near a river.
8. The capital was built on ten square miles of government land.
9. Pierre L'Enfant was the designer of the project.
10. This famous engineer planned the city.

Directions: Circle the simple subject in each sentence. Then complete the puzzle with those words. (Hint: Each word can fit correctly in only one place.)

11. Many tourists visit Washington, D.C. every year.
12. This city with its famous buildings has many attractions.
13. The President's home is called the White House.
14. Visitors tour its many public rooms.
15. The first President in the White House was John Adams.

Notes for Home: Your child identified subjects and predicates in sentences and added information to form complete sentences from sentence fragments. ***Home Activity:*** Say some sentence fragments to your child. *(Answered a question.)* Have him or her add information to form complete sentences.

Name ____________________

REVIEW

Subjects and Predicates

Directions: In each sentence below, underline the complete subject once and the complete predicate twice.

1. Some people think that what you wear says a lot about who you are.
2. Students in my school seem to believe these ideas about clothes.
3. They think the latest styles identify a "cool" person.
4. The fads are sometimes expensive and uncomfortable.
5. Many people wear them anyway.
6. I don't think clothes are all that important.
7. I believe that clothing tells only about the outside of a person.
8. Some schools have dress codes that tell what students can wear.
9. Students in other schools wear uniforms that all look alike.
10. Students in those schools may focus more on what's inside the people they meet.

Directions: Write sentences that include the following simple subjects and predicates. Remember to begin each sentence with a capital letter and end each one with a punctuation mark.

11. style is

____

____

12. people spend

____

____

13. rules would be

____

____

14. friends dress

____

____

15. I would like

____

____

Notes for Home: Your child identified simple and complete subjects and predicates and wrote sentences using simple subjects and predicates. ***Home Activity:*** Challenge your child to complete a sentence that is missing a subject or a predicate.

Name ______________________________

Independent and Dependent Clauses

A sentence part that has a subject and a predicate and makes sense by itself is called an **independent clause.**

Hal likes to dive, and he is also a good swimmer.
independent clause — independent clause

A **dependent clause** also has a subject and a predicate, but it does not make sense by itself. It cannot stand alone as a sentence.

Before he dives in an unfamiliar spot, he checks it for depth and for other safety factors.
dependent clause

Directions: Write **I** if the underlined words are an independent clause. Write **D** if the underlined words are a dependent clause.

______ **1.** Carlos bought new shoes, but he didn't really like them.

______ **2.** Since the shoes had high backs, they were just like other kids' shoes.

______ **3.** Because they were so high, the backs of the shoes hurt Carlos's feet.

______ **4.** The other kids would laugh at him if he didn't wear shoes like theirs.

______ **5.** Blisters develop when your shoes rub the wrong place.

______ **6.** Try on a lot of shoes before you buy a pair.

______ **7.** Choose carefully, and don't buy anything uncomfortable.

______ **8.** Think for yourself, or you'll wish you did!

______ **9.** If you don't think for yourself, you're acting like a sheep.

______ **10.** A sheep will follow another sheep, even if it walks into danger.

Notes for Home: Your child identified independent clauses, which make complete sentences by themselves, and dependent clauses, which must be parts of longer sentences. ***Home Activity:*** Have your child mark and identify clauses in a newspaper article.

Name ______________________________

Independent and Dependent Clauses

Directions: Write **I** if the underlined words are an independent clause. Write **D** if the underlined words are a dependent clause.

__________ **1.** Lily made a wish that her casts would come off soon.

__________ **2.** Lily would practice before autumn came.

__________ **3.** After school started, she could play again.

__________ **4.** Lily watched the game, but she was feeling sad.

__________ **5.** Before she was injured, she had been a very active girl.

Directions: Add an independent clause to complete each sentence. Write the new sentence on the lines.

6. If Lily looks eager to talk,

____

____

7. She could coach other players now, or

____

____

8. Lily can move around on crutches, and

____

____

9. When she calls friends on the phone,

____

____

10. Because she likes mystery films,

____

____

Write a Description

On a separate sheet of paper, write a description of a good friend. Use at least three sentences that contain independent clauses.

Notes for Home: Your child identified independent clauses, which can be sentences by themselves, and dependent clauses, which must be parts of longer sentences. ***Home Activity:*** Write some simple sentences. Have your child add a dependent clause to each one.

Name ______________________

RETEACHING

Independent and Dependent Clauses

Underline each independent clause once. Underline each dependent clause twice.

1. Although our house might seem strange, my family lives a happy life.
2. We grow our own food, and we read lots of books.
3. I've thought about moving back into an apartment, but I would miss being outside.

An **independent clause** is a sentence part that has a subject and a predicate. It can make sense as a complete sentence. A **dependent clause** is a sentence part that has a subject and a predicate, but it cannot make sense as a complete sentence.

Directions: Write **I** if the underlined group of words is an independent clause. Write **D** if the underlined group of words is a dependent clause.

______ 1. It was my first day at the new school, and I wasn't sure how other kids would react to my name.

______ 2. When I sat down at my new desk, I looked around at my classmates' faces.

______ 3. Everyone looked pretty nice, but no one had spoken to me.

______ 4. Because I was a little shy, I hoped someone would introduce herself or himself to me.

______ 5. My teacher started taking attendance, and I listened to her.

Directions: Add an independent clause to complete each sentence. Write each new sentence on the line.

6. When the teacher said, "Sunshine Bluebird McGuire,"

____

____

7. Although I was nervous about what my new classmates might say,

____

____

Notes for Home: Your child used independent clauses, which make complete sentences by themselves, and dependent clauses, which must be parts of longer sentences. ***Home Activity:*** Together, listen to a news report on the radio. Have your child identify independent and dependent clauses.

Name ______________________________

Independent and Dependent Clauses

Directions: Add an independent clause to complete each sentence. Write each new sentence on the lines.

1. As soon as I was old enough,

____

____

2. When I have my next birthday,

____

____

3. Although I would rather be with my friends,

____

____

4. Because I like to do my best in school,

____

____

Directions: Add a dependent clause to complete each sentence. Write each new sentence on the lines.

5. ______________________________, I will probably go on to college.

____

____

6. ______________________________, I like to spend time thinking about my day.

____

____

7. ______________________________, we travel or spend time doing work around the house.

____

____

8. ______________________________, my sister and I have become very good at sharing.

____

____

Notes for Home: Your child wrote independent and dependent clauses in sentences. ***Home Activity:*** Together, look at "April's Mud." Have your child identify independent and dependent clauses in sentences in the story.

Name ______________________________

REVIEW

Independent and Dependent Clauses

Directions: Read each sentence. Underline all the independent clauses once. Underline all the dependent clauses twice.

1. If you like learning about different cultures, museums are a great place to start.
2. Some museums show the culture and history of one group of people, but others show many different groups.
3. When you visit California, stop by the California African American Museum in Los Angeles.
4. You can learn about African American culture at this museum, because it has many exhibits by and about African Americans.
5. After you visit there, you could also go to the Museum of African American History in Detroit, Michigan.
6. This museum includes a large model of a slave ship, but it also has modern displays.

Directions: Add an independent clause to each dependent clause below.

7. If you are interested in cultural history, ______________________________
____
____
8. Whenever I visit there, ______________________________
____
____
9. Because I'm interested in American Indian history, ______________________________
____
____
10. As I learn more about different cultures, ______________________________
____
____

Notes for Home: Your child identified dependent and independent clauses and wrote independent clauses. ***Home Activity:*** Ask your child to write sentences about a favorite tradition and identify the dependent and independent clauses in the sentences.

Name ______________________________

Compound and Complex Sentences

Compound sentences and **complex sentences** help make writing more interesting.

A **compound sentence** contains two independent clauses joined with a comma and a word such as *or, and,* or *but.*

A woman wove rugs, and her husband made drums.
(A woman wove rugs = independent clause; her husband made drums = independent clause)

A **complex sentence** contains one independent clause and one or more dependent clauses. The independent and dependent clauses are joined with words such as *if, because,* or *when.*

Because she dyes her own yarn, she weaves brightly colored rugs.
(Because she dyes her own yarn = dependent clause; she weaves brightly colored rugs = independent clause)

Directions: Write whether each sentence is **compound** or **complex.**

______________ **1.** Kit likes to cook, and she likes to travel.

______________ **2.** Wherever she goes, she collects recipes.

______________ **3.** Her collection is huge, but the recipes are all different.

______________ **4.** After Kit comes home, her friends love to visit.

______________ **5.** Since Kit loves company, she cooks her own favorite foods, which are very tasty.

______________ **6.** Kit buys spices from around the world, and she brings them home.

______________ **7.** She likes spicy food, but her friends don't care for it.

______________ **8.** If she cooks for herself, Kit uses many spices.

______________ **9.** Whenever she travels, she eats spicy food.

______________ **10.** While she's here at home, Kit will write a cookbook.

Notes for Home: Your child identified compound and complex sentences. ***Home Activity:*** Give your child a simple sentence, and challenge him or her to change it into a compound sentence or a complex sentence.

Compound and Complex Sentences

Directions: Write whether each sentence is **compound** or **complex.**

__________ **1.** Anthropologists are scientists, and human beings are their field of study.

__________ **2.** Since each culture is different, a scientist may explore just one.

__________ **3.** Some cultures are known for their music, but no culture is known for music alone.

__________ **4.** When I see a piece of art, I think about who made it.

__________ **5.** You can learn about a culture if you look at its food, music, and art.

Directions: Choose the group of words in ( ) that will best complete each sentence. Write the complete sentence on the line, adding a comma if necessary.

6. Try Vietnamese beef stew _____.
(and enjoy its spicy flavor/although I don't have a recipe)

____

7. If a feast is held, _____.
(and at certain other times/a culture may have a special dance)

____

8. Cultures new to you are interesting, _____.
(because someone invites you/and learning about them is fun)

____

9. When we study another culture, _____.
(and its people study us, in turn/we also learn about ourselves)

____

10. When you try another culture's specialties, _____.
(some dishes may seem different/but never do this in a hurry)

____

Write an E-mail Message

Using a computer or a separate sheet of paper, write an e-mail message to tell a friend about a culture you find interesting. Include both compound and complex sentences.

Notes for Home: Your child identified compound sentences and complex sentences. ***Home Activity:*** Ask your child to point out compound and complex sentences in newspaper or magazine articles.

Name ______________________________

Compound and Complex Sentences

Underline each independent clause.

1. Jonathan wants to travel to Milan, but he is too busy this month.

Underline the dependent clause once and the independent clause twice.

2. Although I felt nervous, I took the test anyway.

A **compound sentence** contains two independent clauses joined with a comma and a word such as *and, or,* or *but.* A **complex sentence** contains one dependent clause and one independent clause joined by a word such as *if, because,* or *although.*

Directions: Write whether each sentence is **compound** or **complex.**

____________ **1.** The sign goes here, and the banner goes there.

____________ **2.** While you direct traffic, John can do his job.

____________ **3.** Sue is in charge of books, but she's not here yet.

____________ **4.** If you cover for her, I'll give you a hand.

____________ **5.** This is a big event, and nothing must go wrong.

____________ **6.** I'm weary too, but we don't have time to rest.

____________ **7.** Did Mrs. Ellis donate the hat, or was it Mr. West?

____________ **8.** Because we are doing so well, we may be able to close early.

____________ **9.** The shoes are selling fast, but no one's buying ties.

____________ **10.** This suit cost ten dollars, but it's worth more.

____________ **11.** That red hat looks good, but that one looks better.

____________ **12.** You should go home if you aren't going to help.

____________ **13.** May I help you, or are you just browsing?

____________ **14.** Although we haven't marked the price on that one, we'll sell it to you for five dollars.

____________ **15.** We have done very well, but let's stay open for another half an hour.

Notes for Home: Your child identified compound and complex sentences. ***Home Activity:*** Have your child use this page to explain to you the differences between compound and complex sentences.

Name ______________________________

Compound and Complex Sentences

Directions: Write whether each sentence is **compound** or **complex.**

______________ **1.** Math is my favorite subject, but my grades are often low.

______________ **2.** My teacher helps and encourages me when I come to her with questions.

______________ **3.** If I spend a little extra time on my math homework each night, I will understand more of the discussion in class the next day.

______________ **4.** Memorizing is hard for me, and I forget important rules.

______________ **5.** I must study hard, or my grades will not improve.

______________ **6.** Because I am a hard worker, I know I will get better in time.

Directions: Add a word such as *and, or,* or *but* and more information to complete each compound sentence.

7. It is important to do your work carefully ______________________________

____

8. I like to write stories ______________________________

____

9. My teacher is very patient ______________________________

____

Directions: Add a dependent clause to complete each complex sentence. Write the new sentence on the lines.

10. ______________________________, we can skip doing homework one night.

____

____

11. ______________________________, my friends went to the movie without me.

____

____

12. ______________________________, I will be very happy.

____

____

Notes for Home: Your child identified and completed compound and complex sentences. ***Home Activity:*** Have your child read a newspaper or magazine article and mark two compound sentences and two complex sentences. Then have him or her make up another one of each.

Name ______________________________

Compound and Complex Sentences

REVIEW

Directions: Write whether each sentence is compound or complex.

______________ **1.** While a customer is eating, he suddenly cannot breathe.

______________ **2.** He turns blue, and his finger points to his throat.

______________ **3.** The Heimlich Maneuver could save his life, and fortunately the waitress knows how to perform the maneuver.

______________ **4.** As she stands behind the customer, she wraps her arms around his waist.

______________ **5.** When she presses quickly beneath his ribs, the stuck piece of food finally comes out.

Directions: Add an independent clause to the first two sentences to make them compound sentences. Add independent clauses to the last three sentences to make them complex sentences. Write the complete sentences on the lines.

6. (compound sentence) Life is full of emergencies, and _____.

____

____

7. (compound sentence) You should learn CPR and the Heimlich Maneuver, but _____.

____

____

8. (complex) _____ if you couldn't help someone in need.

____

____

9. (complex) If you can swim, _____.

____

____

10. (complex) When there is an emergency, _____.

____

____

Notes for Home: Your child identified and wrote compound and complex sentences. ***Home Activity:*** Give your child two simple sentences and challenge him or her to combine them into a compound sentence.

Name ______________________________

Combining Sentences

If two sentences have different subjects but the same predicate, you can combine the subjects to form a **compound subject** by using the word *and.*

Simple sentences: Jason gazed at the stars above. His sister gazed at the stars above.

Compound subject: Jason and his sister gazed at the stars above.

If two sentences have the same subject and different predicates, you can combine the predicates to form a **compound predicate** by using the word *and.*

Simple sentences: Marika waited for the bus. Marika watched the darkening sky.

Compound predicate: Marika waited for the bus and watched the darkening sky.

If two sentences have related ideas, you can combine the sentences to form a **compound sentence** by using a comma and words like *or, but,* or *and.*

Simple sentences: I was nervous. My knees were knocking.

Compound sentence: I was nervous, and my knees were knocking.

Directions: Combine each pair of sentences to form a compound subject, a compound predicate, or a compound sentence. Use the joining word *and.*

1. Sook and Lin Yu were frightened. Sook and Lin Yu wanted to go home.

____

____

2. They were in the woods. They saw how dark it was.

____

____

3. Sook saw a mysterious shape. Lin Yu saw a mysterious shape too.

____

____

4. The shape came forward. It was huge.

____

____

5. Sook shivered. Lin Yu shook.

____

____

Notes for Home: Your child has learned to combine sentences. ***Home Activity:*** Using a favorite book, ask your child to show you how to combine sentences.

Name ______________________________

Combining Sentences

Directions: Combine each pair of sentences to form a compound subject, a compound predicate, or a compound sentence. Use the joining word *or, and,* or *but.*

1. Tara smiled happily. Tara hummed a little song.

____

2. Tara planned to have fun. Her friends planned to have fun.

____

3. They would swim. They would dive.

____

4. The parking lot was empty. The beach was empty.

____

5. Huge waves came in. Huge waves broke on the sand.

____

6. Tara felt nervous. Her friends yelled happily.

____

7. The waves were big. Tara stepped backward.

____

8. Tara sat down on the sand. Her friends went wading.

____

9. A wave crashed down. Angie disappeared.

____

10. The water grew calmer. Angie stood up.

____

Write a Paragraph

Write a paragraph to finish the story of Tara and her friends. Then look for sentences you can combine to make your writing more interesting.

Notes for Home: Your child combined short sentences to form longer, more interesting sentences. ***Home Activity:*** Ask your child to explain various ways of combining sentences. Then, together, examine newspaper ads, looking for sentences that can be combined.

Name ______________________

Combining Sentences

Combine each pair of sentences. Write each new sentence.

1. Margaret walked home. Peter walked home.

____

2. Margaret went to the library. Margaret stopped by the store.

____

3. They left for the airport early. They got stuck in traffic.

____

Form a **compound subject** by combining two sentences with the same predicate but different subjects. Form a **compound predicate** by combining two sentences that have the same subject but different predicates. Form a **compound sentence** by combining two simple sentences that have related ideas.

Directions: Combine each pair of sentences to form a sentence with a compound subject or a compound predicate, or to form a compound sentence. Use the joining word *or, and,* or *but.* Write each new sentence on the line.

1. Jane Wilkinson is new at Kennedy School this year. Ray Wilkinson is new at Kennedy School this year.

____

____

2. Jane and Ray don't know anyone at school. They would like to make new friends.

____

____

3. My brother invites Ray to club meetings. My brother's friends invite Ray to club meetings.

____

4. Carole opened the newspaper. Carole read about Taylor and Ushma.

____

5. They had entered a literary contest. They had tied for first prize.

____

Notes for Home: Your child wrote compound sentences and sentences with compound subjects and compound predicates. ***Home Activity:*** Write simple sentences about your family. Have your child combine them to form compound sentences or sentences with compound subjects or predicates.

Name ______________________

Combining Sentences

Directions: Combine each pair of sentences to form a sentence with a compound subject or a compound predicate, or to form a compound sentence. Use the joining word *and, but,* or *or.* Write each new sentence.

1. I am the oldest child in my family. I am not the tallest.

____

2. My younger brother Josh is taller than I am. My younger brother Sam is taller than I am.

____

3. I have more responsibilities than my brothers and sister. I do more chores than my brothers and sister.

____

4. My mother expects me to make snacks for my siblings after school. I have to make sure they start their homework right away.

____

____

5. I return our library books on my way home from school. I buy fresh bread for dinner.

____

____

6. My dad broke his leg last year. He wasn't able to do many of the things around the house that he normally does.

____

____

7. The doctor said he had to stay in bed. He could sit in a chair with his leg elevated and watch TV.

____

____

8. My brothers wanted to be helpful to our dad. They weren't sure how.

____

9. We had a big celebration for my dad the day his cast was taken off. We made a cake for my dad the day his cast was taken off.

____

____

Notes for Home: Your child wrote compound sentences and sentences with compound subjects and predicates. ***Home Activity:*** Have your child look at a story that he or she enjoyed as a young child. Have your child combine simple sentences from the story to form compound sentences.

Name ______________________________

REVIEW

Subjects

Directions: Underline the complete subject in each sentence. Then circle the simple subject. (There may be more than one simple subject in a sentence.)

1. All crows have feathers of a glossy black color.

2. The hooded crow has touches of gray as well.

3. North America and Eurasia are home to the most common kinds of crows.

4. Eurasia includes both Europe and Asia.

5. The crow's name comes from its "caw" or "craw" sound.

6. Grains, berries, insects, dead animals, and other birds' eggs are its favorite foods.

7. Fifteen to twenty years is not an unusual life span for a crow in captivity.

8. This big, noisy, sociable bird is extremely smart.

9. Some owners of pet crows have taught their birds to "speak" on command.

10. Other crows in laboratories have been taught to count up to three or four.

Directions: Use each of the following subjects in a sentence of your own. Write the sentence on the line. Then circle the simple subject.

11. A group of big black birds

____

____

12. A nest full of robin's eggs

____

____

13. One of the hungry birds

____

____

14. A second black bird

____

____

15. A female robin and then the male

____

____

Notes for Home: Your child recognized simple and complete subjects and used them in sentences. ***Home Activity:*** Look through a newspaper, magazine, or book with your child. Encourage your child to find the simple and complete subjects of sentences.

Name ______________________________________

Proper Nouns and Common Nouns

A noun names one or more persons, places, or things. (Things include ideas.) A **proper noun** is the name of a *particular* person, place, or thing: *Anne D. Gray, Texas, Tuesday,* and *Dr. Fiorenza* are proper nouns.

A proper noun, such as *Martin Luther King Jr. School,* may consist of more than one word. Begin each important word in a proper noun with a capital letter.

Nouns that are not proper nouns are called **common nouns.** A common noun does not name any particular person, place, or thing. The words *sister, state,* and *day* are common nouns. Common nouns are not capitalized.

Directions: Underline the nouns in each sentence. If a noun is a proper noun, underline it twice.

1. A flock of crows lives near the open meadow.
2. Each morning joggers can hear these birds all over Central Park.
3. When Mrs. Wall is walking her terrier nearby, the crows sound an alarm.
4. "Mr. Jet" is my name for the crow with the harshest voice.
5. His nest is high in the tallest evergreen near Turtle Pond.
6. Students from Barnard College check their guides to local birds.
7. Roger Tory Peterson wrote five guides for birdwatchers.
8. Do ravens really live at the Tower of London?
9. In Manhattan, falcons lay their eggs on the ledges of skyscrapers.
10. Gyrfalcons are found at the Arctic Circle, not in New York City.

Directions: Write **C** if the noun is a common noun. Write **P** if the noun is a proper noun. If it is a proper noun, rewrite it correctly on the line.

11. field ____________________
12. hoyt park ____________________
13. thanksgiving ____________________
14. binoculars ____________________
15. mr. a. p. finney ____________________

Notes for Home: Your child identified proper nouns and common nouns. ***Home Activity:*** Just for fun, challenge your child to try to speak for five minutes without using *any* nouns.

Proper Nouns and Common Nouns

Directions: Underline the nouns in each sentence. If a noun is a proper noun, underline it twice.

1. Our family visited Maine this summer.
2. The trip began with a drive up the coast to a town called Camden.
3. Kennebunkport and Bangor are full of shops and restaurants.
4. The next stop was at Acadia National Park.
5. Outstanding features of the trip were Thunder Hole and Cadillac Mountain.

Directions: Rewrite each sentence on the lines below. Capitalize all proper nouns.

6. The ocean was spectacular that day, and acadia park was beautiful.

____

____

7. Dad drove through washington county to new brunswick, canada.

____

____

8. The bay of fundy is an unusual body of water.

____

____

9. Because of the shape of this bay, which is in canada, the tide comes in suddenly.

____

____

10. A 42-foot wall of water rushes in from the atlantic ocean in just minutes!

____

____

Write About a Place

Write a paragraph or two describing the town or city where you live. Name a few points of interest, such as parks or buildings, and explain why they are important. Use at least three common nouns and three proper nouns.

Notes for Home: Your child identified proper nouns and common nouns and capitalized proper nouns. ***Home Activity:*** Together, write a variety of common and proper nouns on slips of paper. Take turns with your child, drawing slips and using the nouns in sentences.

Name ______________________________

Proper Nouns and Common Nouns

RETEACHING

Draw a line to join each common noun on the left with a proper noun on the right.

Common Noun	**Proper Noun**
inventor	New Jersey
month	Thomas Alva Edison
state	February

A **common noun** names any of a kind of person, place, or thing. A **proper noun** names a particular person, place, or thing. Proper nouns always begin with capital letters.

Directions: Write **common noun** or **proper noun** to describe the underlined word.

1. Thomas Edison invented the lightbulb. ______________
2. Thomas Alva Edison was born in Ohio in 1847. ______________
3. He was educated at home by his mother. ______________
4. At age twelve he was a newsboy. ______________
5. Edison later worked on a train in Michigan. ______________

Directions: Underline the common nouns and proper nouns in each sentence.

6. Edison patented over a thousand inventions.
7. Where did the busy inventor work in America?
8. The laboratory was in New Jersey.
9. His phonograph was famous in Europe.
10. Thomas Edison helped to invent movies.

Directions: Copy the nouns you underlined in items 6–10. Write each one in the correct column.

Common Nouns	**Proper Nouns**
11. ______________	12. ______________
13. ______________	14. ______________
15. ______________	16. ______________
17. ______________	18. ______________
19. ______________	20. ______________

Notes for Home: Your child identified and categorized common nouns and proper nouns. ***Home Activity:*** Together, write a list of nouns that name persons, places, and things in your home. Have your child capitalize proper nouns correctly.

Name ______________________________

Proper Nouns and Common Nouns

Directions: Read the paragraph. Write each underlined noun in the correct column.

Do you know about the huge statues of heads on Easter Island? Easter Island is located in the South Pacific west of Chile. Scientists do not know much about the background of the statues. There are more than 600 of these giant heads with long ears. Jacob Roggeven first saw the carved giants in 1722. The heads weigh fifty tons and do not look like the Polynesians on this Pacific island.

Common Nouns	Proper Nouns
1. ______________	2. ______________
3. ______________	4. ______________
5. ______________	6. ______________
7. ______________	8. ______________
9. ______________	10. ______________

Directions: Underline each common noun once and each proper noun twice.

11. The statues on Easter Island are made of red stone.
12. Some statues are over 40 feet and weigh 90 tons.
13. Islanders carved the statues from the rock of extinct volcanoes.
14. The builders of these figures are still unknown to the experts.
15. Thor Heyerdahl sailed to Easter Island on a raft.
16. This explorer from Norway studied the currents of the Pacific Ocean.
17. Heyerdahl wrote an interesting book about the monuments.
18. This book contains ideas about the mystery of the lonely island in the Pacific.
19. Today its population includes many Chileans.
20. The librarian will find the book for the class.

Write an Announcement

On a separate sheet of paper, write an announcement about a discovery you made, such as an unusual stone or a special place. Before you begin writing, think about what you were doing right before you made the discovery. Then start to write. Tell what you discovered and where you found it. Use common and proper nouns.

Notes for Home: Your child has identified common nouns and proper nouns and capitalized proper nouns correctly. ***Home Activity:*** Have your child read his or her announcement. Then have him or her underline common nouns and circle proper nouns.

Nouns

REVIEW

Directions: Underline each noun in the sentences that follow. Underline proper nouns twice.

1. My Aunt Fay and her children, Alana and Nathan, were taking a bus from New Hampshire to Cape Cod.
2. From the bus, Nathan pointed out Boston and Plymouth.
3. Of course, Plymouth and Plymouth Rock are famous as the landing place of the Pilgrims in the seventeenth century.
4. The passengers felt a sudden jolt, and the bus went into a skid along Route 95.
5. Fortunately, Officer Eileen Regan and Officer Jamal Davis were on the scene quickly, and no one suffered serious injury.

Directions: Write each sentence correctly. Remember to capitalize all proper nouns.

6. The famous mt. everest lies in the himalayan mountains in asia.

____

____

7. In 1953, edmund hillary and tenzing norgay became the first climbers to reach the soaring peak.

____

____

8. Thousands have climbed mt. mcKinley in north america and mt. kilimanjaro in africa.

____

____

9. Hundreds of climbers from europe, the americas, japan, and other parts of the world have died in these attempts.

____

____

10. A chilling book by jon krakauer tells of the twelve climbers who died climbing mt. everest in may 1996.

____

____

Notes for Home: Your child identified and used common and proper nouns in sentences. ***Home Activity:*** Take a walk with your child. Encourage your child to list the people, places, and things you see, using common and proper nouns.

Name ______________________________________

Plural Nouns

A noun that names more than one person, place, thing, or idea is a **plural noun.**

Regular Nouns

- Add **-s** or **-es** to most nouns to make them plural: fork, forks.
- Add **-es** to nouns ending in **ch, sh, x, z, s** or **ss:** match, matches; wish, wishes; box, boxes; buzz, buzzes; bus, buses; success, successes.
- If a noun ends in a **vowel** followed by **y,** add **-s.** If a noun ends in a **consonant** and **y,** change the **y** to **i** and add **-es:** journey, journeys; lady, ladies.

Irregular Nouns

- Some nouns have the same singular and plural form: elk/elk; deer/deer.
- Some nouns change the spelling of the word to form the plural: child, children; ox, oxen.
- You can form the plurals of some nouns ending in **f** or **fe** by changing **f** or **fe** to **v** and adding **-es:** wolf, wolves; knife, knives.
- Add **-s** to certain nouns that end in **f:** roof, roofs; chief, chiefs.
- Add **-s** to nearly all nouns that end in **ff:** sheriff, sheriffs.
- Add **-s** to nouns ending in a **vowel** and **o:** patio, patios; stereo, stereos.
- Check the dictionary for plurals of nouns ending in a consonant followed by **o:** photo, photos; piano, pianos; hero, heroes; tomato, tomatoes.

Directions: Write the plural form of each underlined noun. Use a dictionary if you need help.

____________________ **1.** Kelly saw a thief, but not the kind a sheriff would arrest.

____________________ **2.** The fox was holding a large mouse in its jaw.

____________________ **3.** The bandit couldn't unlock the latch of the gate.

____________________ **4.** It managed to slip under the fence.

____________________ **5.** It ran across the vegetable garden.

____________________ **6.** The fox would feed its baby before eating.

____________________ **7.** The sheep in the field was alarmed.

____________________ **8.** It stamped its hoof in fear.

____________________ **9.** It wished a hero would come to the rescue!

____________________ **10.** High above the roof, an osprey wished it had caught the mouse.

Notes for Home: Your child wrote plural nouns. ***Home Activity:*** Look through a catalog or an illustrated encyclopedia with your child. Ask your child to tell you how to form plurals of the names of objects pictured.

Name ______________________________

Plural Nouns

Directions: Write the plural form of each noun in ( ). Use a dictionary if you need help.

______________ **1.** The (cliff) towered above the two climbers.

______________ **2.** (Patch) of blue could be seen between the rocky slopes.

______________ **3.** Were those (elk) scrambling over the rocks?

______________ **4.** Even as (child), the climbers had dreamed about this mountain!

______________ **5.** They also had heard many (story) about its dangers.

______________ **6.** They were not (hero), just two people trying to reach its peak.

______________ **7.** Therefore, they were well equipped with (ax) and other tools.

______________ **8.** Some unpleasant (surprise) awaited them, however.

______________ **9.** Soon their (life) would be in great danger.

______________ **10.** Would they reach camp before the (sky) turned dark?

Directions: Write five sentences. Use the plural form of one noun in the box in each sentence. Use all five nouns.

journey	foot	challenge	spy	knife

11. ______________________________

12. ______________________________

13. ______________________________

14. ______________________________

15. ______________________________

Write a TV News Report

Think of a real or fictional person who was caught in a dangerous situation and survived. On a separate sheet of paper, write a short report for the TV evening news. Include at least three plural nouns in your report.

Notes for Home: Your child wrote the plural forms of various nouns. ***Home Activity:*** Ask your child to use a book or a magazine to find plural nouns and tell you the singular form of each one.

Name ______________________________

Possessive Nouns

Directions: Rewrite each underlined phrase to show possession. Write the new phrase on the line.

______________ **1.** The noses of the animals were lifted to the wind.

______________ **2.** Heavy with leaves, the branches of trees creaked and swayed.

______________ **3.** Even the tails of the squirrels twitched nervously.

______________ **4.** All the animals could sense the threat of the storm.

______________ **5.** The waters of the river flowed fast and choppy.

______________ **6.** A frightened deer ran to the edge of the water and tried to cross.

______________ **7.** The legs of the deer became caught in a swirling branch.

______________ **8.** Soon the cries of the creature rang through the forest.

______________ **9.** Fortunately, a cabin for campers stood near the river.

______________ **10.** Because of the bravery of the people, the life of the deer was saved.

Write a Description

On a separate sheet of paper, write a description of a storm and how it makes you feel. Use colorful words in your description. Use at least three possessive nouns in your description.

Notes for Home: Your child wrote the possessive forms of nouns. ***Home Activity:*** Write a variety of nouns on small slips of paper. Take turns with your child, choosing the slips and spelling or writing the singular and plural possessive forms of the nouns.

Name ______________________

Possessive Nouns

Underline the possessive nouns. Write the nouns.

1. Sue's smile was joyful. ______________________
2. The seals' barks were heard outside. ______________________
3. Children's laughter rang in the air. ______________________

A **possessive noun** shows ownership. Add an apostrophe **(')** and **-s** to spell the possessive form of a singular noun. Add only an apostrophe to spell the possessive form of a plural noun that ends with **-s.** Add an apostrophe and **-s** to spell the possessive form of a plural noun that does not end in **-s.**

Directions: Underline the possessive nouns.

1. The bear's food is being prepared.
2. Lions' roars could be heard throughout the zoo.
3. The keeper's pride in the big cats was clear.
4. The girls ran quickly to the alligators' pits.
5. The boys laughed at the hippopotamus's big yawn.
6. Mr. Morris was fascinated by the monkey's actions.
7. He drew the children's attention to the bears.
8. The sleeping cub's face shone with contentment.
9. The tourists' guide pointed to the cub.

Directions: Write the possessive form of the noun in ( ).

10. The ______________ laughter woke the bear. (men)
11. Look at the ______________ sharp claw. (animal)
12. The ______________ eyes opened wide. (visitors)
13. It walked to the ______________ corner for a nap. (cage)
14. The ______________ directions helped us. (guide)
15. The ______________ cage has a tree trunk with branches. (snake)
16. The ______________ habitat has a lake. (deer)

Notes for Home: Your child used possessive forms of singular and plural nouns. ***Home Activity:*** Have your child make a list of friends, family members, and families' last names. Have him or her write sentences, using the lists to write possessive nouns.

Name ______________________________

Possessive Nouns

Directions: Write in the blank the posessive form of the noun in ( ).

1. ______________ population is enormous. (China)
2. China is the ______________ third largest country in land area. (world)
3. This ______________ history dates from 3500 years ago. (country)
4. Early ______________ name for China was "Zhonghua." (scholars)
5. The ______________ meaning is "central land." (word)
6. Their homeland seemed like the ______________ center. (Earth)
7. The ______________ height protected the land. (mountains)
8. The ______________ shores formed its eastern border. (seas)
9. We listened eargerly to the ______________ stories about China. (travelers)

Directions: Rewrite each underlined phrase so that it contains a possessive noun.

10. Chinese civilization was influenced by <u>the ideas of many philosophers</u>.

____

11. Confucius was <u>the son of a noble</u>.

____

12. <u>The beliefs of this man</u> taught love, wisdom, and sincerity.

____

13. Respect for parents was important in <u>the lessons of his students</u>.

____

14. Today his ideas still influence <u>the customs of China</u>.

____

15. <u>The education of children</u> is based on Confucius's teaching.

____

Write a Travel Brochure

On a separate sheet of paper, write a travel brochure for a country you would like to visit. Describe the weather, the people, and must-see places to explore. Use possessive nouns in some of your sentences.

Notes for Home: Your child used possessive forms of singular and plural nouns in sentences. ***Home Activity:*** Together, make a list of places your child often goes. Have your child use possessive forms of the place names to write sentences about what can be found there.

Name ______________________________

REVIEW

Sentence Punctuation

Directions: Write **C** if the sentence has correct end punctuation. If the punctuation is incorrect, write the correct punctuation on the line.

1. Do you have an animal shelter in your town. _____
2. What a great job those shelters do! _____
3. They rescue and take in animals of all kinds, especially cats and dogs? _____
4. Please answer this question? _____
5. Did you adopt your cat from the local shelter? _____
6. The shelter was full of adorable animals. _____
7. How hard it must have been to choose one animal? _____
8. How long did it take you to make up your mind? _____

Directions: Read each sentence. Some are compound sentences. Add a comma to each compound sentence. Then add the correct end punctuation to all sentences.

9. The day was hot and we decided to drive to the beach
10. We packed our bathing suits and a delicious picnic lunch
11. We had to wait for Leroy and Anna was a little late too
12. Finally we were in the car and on our way
13. How excited we were about going to the beach
14. What is in the middle of the road ahead
15. It might be a small horse or a sheep or it could be a large dog
16. My mom slowed the car and we saw a big, dirty, tired dog
17. Should we stop or should we continue driving
18. We wanted to keep going but we could not abandon that poor animal
19. What a smart decision we made
20. We never got to the beach but we did eventually get the best pet in the world

Notes for Home: Your child added punctuation marks to the ends of sentences and added commas between parts of compound sentences. ***Home Activity:*** Challenge your child to explain the reason for the punctuation in several sentences in favorite books or magazines.

Name ____________________

Commas with Nouns in Series and in Direct Address

A **comma** is a punctuation mark that is used to set off a word or a group of words from other words in the same sentence. In this way, a comma helps to make the meaning of a sentence clear.

Three or more words (such as nouns) or groups of words listed together in a sentence are called a **series.** A comma is used after each item in the series except the last.

Mike, Sam, and Tammy went to Stewart Beach Aquarium.
The three friends had peanut butter and jelly sandwiches, apples, and juice for lunch.

One or two commas are used to set off the names of people who are directly addressed in speech or writing. This use of a noun is called **direct address.**

Mike, do you know which bus goes to the aquarium?
I think, Tammy, that it is the M17 bus.
Do you know for sure, Sam?

Directions: Add commas to each sentence to set off nouns used in a series or in direct address.

1. Eleanor Joe and Terry work at Stewart Beach Aquarium.
2. Eleanor gives tours on Fridays Saturdays and Sundays.
3. Joe arranges for lectures films and shows.
4. Did you think Terry that my last lecture was clear?
5. The aquarium has been attracting students teachers and tourists.
6. When is the next showing of the film about dolphins Joe?
7. Terry is one of the people who feed the dolphins porpoises and seals.
8. Joe please finish the new schedule by Friday.
9. Stingrays sharks manatees and squids are just a few of the creatures that you can see at the aquarium.
10. Stewart Beach Aquarium is easy to reach by train bus or car.

Notes for Home: Your child added commas to nouns in a series and in direct address. ***Home Activity:*** Say sentences in which people are spoken to directly by name. Ask your child which word the comma should follow.

Name ______________________

Commas with Nouns in Series and in Direct Address

Directions: Add commas to each sentence to set off nouns used in a series or in direct address.

1. Paul do you remember that terrible storm three summers ago?
2. It rained on Monday Tuesday Wednesday and Thursday.
3. Water got into the attic the cellar and the garage.
4. Were you here that summer Jamal?
5. The storm damaged the house the garden and the new deck.

Directions: Rewrite each sentence below to include a noun in direct address. Use commas as needed.

6. Did I tell you about one downpour that lasted nine days?

____

____

7. TV news stories showed rescuers rowing through flooded areas.

____

____

8. Rivers at flood level threatened people's homes.

____

____

9. The nonstop rain was part of the El Niño effect.

____

10. Yes, this occurred in the spring of 1998.

____

Write a News Article

On a separate sheet of paper, write a brief news article about a strong force in nature, such as a blizzard, hurricane, tornado, or flood. The force can be one that you have experienced or one that you have read about or heard about. Include items in a series. Remember to use commas correctly.

Notes for Home: Your child used commas to separate words listed in a series and to set off the names of people being addressed directly. ***Home Activity:*** Invite your child to write several sentences in which three or more items are listed in a series, using commas to separate them.

Name ______________________________

Commas with Nouns in Series and in Direct Address

RETEACHING

Circle the commas in the sentences below.

1. Alicia, what is an aqueduct?
2. It is a water canal, tunnel, or pipe.
3. I am going to Italy to see them, Veronica.

When you write, use commas:
- to separate words or groups of words in a series;
- to set off the name of a person directly addressed.

Directions: Insert commas where they are needed in the following sentences.

1. Jena what is an aqueduct bridge?
2. It is a structure with arches a road and a canal.
3. It carried water people and goods across a valley.
4. Nancy what is the Aqua Appia?
5. It was the first Roman aqueduct Darla.
6. Nine Roman aqueducts were built in all Judy.
7. Some of them John are still in use.

Directions: Use each set of words to write a new sentence. Use the words as items in a series. Add commas where they belong.

8. June July August

____

____

9. pizza ice cream potato chips

____

____

Notes for Home: Your child used commas in sentences with nouns in series and names directly addressed. ***Home Activity:*** Watch a television news program together. Have your child write sentences in which nouns are used in a series or people are directly addressed. Use sentences from the news program.

Name ______________________________

Commas with Nouns in Series and in Direct Address

Directions: Add commas where needed to the sentences below.

1. Sharon who are the Inuit?
2. They are a group of people who live in areas of Greenland North America and Siberia.
3. They inhabit Baffin Island Banks Island and Victoria Island.
4. Inuit is their name for themselves Gerald.
5. Lisa it means "the people."
6. They arrived in North America after the Native Americans Sandra.
7. Kim do the Inuit people have many dialects?
8. Many stories legends and myths are told in the Inuit language.

Directions: Rewrite each sentence below to include a noun in direct address. You may wish to add other information as well. Use commas as needed.

9. Learning another language is easiest when a person is very young.

____

____

10. Why do you think that is true?

____

____

11. If you would like to understand more about a particular culture and its customs, learning some of the language can be helpful.

____

____

Write a Paragraph

On a separate sheet of paper, write a paragraph about a people or culture you would like to study. Describe some of their customs that you find interesting. You may use an encyclopedia to find information, if you wish.

Notes for Home: Your child used commas in sentences in which people are directly addressed by name. ***Home Activity:*** Have your child write commands for toys or stuffed animals in your home, directly addressing them by name. Your child should use commas in his or her written commands.

Name ______________________________

REVIEW

Subjects and Predicates

Directions: Draw a line between the complete subject and the complete predicate in each sentence. Then underline the simple subject and the simple predicate.

1. Pollution of the oceans occurs in many different ways.
2. Oceanographers are needed in increasing numbers.
3. Such experts possess interests in science, the sea, and adventure.
4. Jacques Costeau was the most famous oceanographer of all.
5. This daring, brilliant scientist exposed the ocean's problems to the world.
6. The field of oceanography includes a number of different specialties.
7. The living creatures of the ocean are studied by marine biologists.
8. Pollution problems might be solved someday by a chemical oceanographer.
9. Underwater photographers record the mysteries below the water.
10. Your special interests will lead you to the fascinating study of the world's oceans.

Directions: Write **S** on the line to the left if the group of words can be a sentence subject. Write **P** if the group of words can be a sentence predicate. Then use each group of words to write a sentence of your own.

________ **11.** animals in the ocean

____

____

________ **12.** can cause terrible damage to the seas

____

____

________ **13.** may be changed forever

____

____

________ **14.** recovery from an oil spill

____

____

________ **15.** the secrets of the ocean

____

Notes for Home: Your child identified and used simple and complete subjects and simple and complete predicates. ***Home Activity:*** Have your child write some sentences about events at school and highlight each simple subject and predicate.

Name ______________________________

Subject-Verb Agreement

To work together, the subject of a sentence and the verb must agree in number. The following rules are for sentences that tell what is happening now, at the present time.

For a singular noun subject, add **-s** or **-es** to most verbs.

Tim lives in Alaska.
His brother writes to him from college.

For a plural noun subject, do **not** add **-s** or **-es** to the verb.

Many people visit Tim.
His grandparents travel to Alaska every year.

For compound subjects joined by *and* or *both,* use the verb form for a plural subject.

Carla and Mary want some of Tim's photos of glaciers.
Both his Alaskan friends and his father collect slides of Alaskan wildlife.

For a singular and a plural noun subject joined by *or, either . . . or,* or *neither . . . nor,* the verb must agree with the subject closer to it.

Neither Tim's friends in Washington nor Mary wants to live in the far north.

Directions: Circle the correct present-tense form of the verb in ( ) to complete each sentence.

1. Tim (spend/spends) much of his time working.
2. He (guide/guides) tours through the Alaskan wilderness.
3. Tim and his sister (work/works) together.
4. Four guides (share/shares) the work.
5. Each guide (own/owns) an equal part of the company.

Directions: Write the correct present-tense form of the verb in ( ) to complete each sentence.

______________ 6. On one tour, visitors (sail) through the Gulf of Alaska.

______________ 7. Sometimes, a humpback whale (swim) into view.

______________ 8. Bald eagles often (soar) above the water.

______________ 9. Many small islands (lie) in the Gulf of Alaska.

______________ 10. Sometimes a tour ship or a cabin cruiser (stop) near one of the islands.

Notes for Home: Your child chose and wrote the verb forms that agree with singular subjects and plural subjects. ***Home Activity:*** Have your child choose a verb. Then ask him or her to use the verb in a sentence with a singular subject and in a sentence with a plural subject.

Name ____________________

Subject-Verb Agreement

Directions: Circle the correct form of the verb in ( ) to complete each sentence.

1. Treasure Salvages Inc. (search/searches) the seas for old sunken ships.
2. The company (find/finds) special maps.
3. First, people (look/looks) for clues to find ships that were lost.
4. Next, boats (survey/surveys) likely areas.
5. Usually, a boat (use/uses) a metal detector to find iron objects left by sunken ships.

Directions: Write the correct present-tense form of the verb in ( ) to complete each sentence.

____________ 6. When divers (locate) a sunken ship, they are very careful.

____________ 7. A diver (take) an interest in more than just gold and silver.

____________ 8. Both valuable coins and others relics of the past (interest) the searchers.

____________ 9. Can either a company or individuals (collect) these artifacts and put them into museums?

____________ 10. People (study) these artifacts for clues about the past.

____________ 11. Scientists (examine) any navigational instruments from the old ship.

____________ 12. Passengers' clothing and personal possessions (tell) much about the owners' social position.

____________ 13. The ship's furnishings or cargo also (provide) information.

____________ 14. A museum exhibit usually (include) items like dishes and knives.

____________ 15. What cargo of ancient times (seem) most interesting to you?

Write a Job Description

Choose one outdoor job, such as forest ranger or lifeguard. On a separate sheet of paper, write three or four sentences that describe ways someone in that job might help to protect our environment. Remember to make your subjects and verbs agree.

Notes for Home: Your child learned how to make verbs agree with subjects. ***Home Activity:*** Say a sentence with a singular subject, such as *Ben cleans up the store.* Then give your child a plural subject and have him or her change the verb to make it agree with the subject.

Subject-Verb Agreement

RETEACHING

Subject	Some Verbs That Agree
I	am, was, walk, search
singular nouns and **she, he, it**	is, was, walks, searches
plural nouns and **we, you, they**	are, were, walk, search

Complete the sentence. Write a subject and a verb that agree. Use words from the chart.

______________ ______________ in the park.
(subject) (verb)

A verb must agree with its subject. Add **-s** or **-es** to most verbs with singular subjects. Do **not** add **-s** or **-es** to verbs with plural subjects.

Directions: Complete each sentence. Write the correct form of the verb in ( ).

1. Mountains ______________ from pressure under the Earth's surface. (forms/form)
2. Some mountains ______________ as volcanoes. (starts/start)
3. Molten rock ______________ through the Earth. (pushes/push)
4. The rock ______________ into lava on the surface of the land. (cools/cool)
5. Sometimes underground forces ______________ folds. (causes/cause)
6. The force ______________ areas of land together. (presses/press)
7. The folds ______________ above the land around them. (projects/project)
8. Trees ______________ smaller near the top. (becomes/become)
9. Foggy mornings ______________ often in the mountains. (occurs/occur)
10. A mountain lion ______________ among the high rocks. (hides/hide)
11. A major mountain range called the Alps ______________ in Europe. (exists/exist)
12. Snow usually ______________ high mountains all year long. (covers/cover)
13. The Himalayas ______________ climbers. (challenges/challenge)
14. I ______________ Edmund Hillary was the first to climb Mt. Everest. (knows/know)

Notes for Home: Your child practiced subject-verb agreement by writing verbs in sentences. ***Home Activity:*** Together, make a list of verbs that are involved in your child's favorite activity. Have him or her write sentences, making sure subjects and verbs agree.

Name ______________________________

Subject-Verb Agreement

Directions: Circle the simple subject. Write the correct form of the verb in ( ) to agree with the subject.

1. Three primary colors ________________ all of the other colors. (creates/create)
2. I ________________ red and blue. (prefers/prefer)
3. The light of every color ________________ in waves. (travel/travels)
4. Red's waves ________________ the furthest. (stretch/stretches)
5. The human eye ________________ the different waves. (distinguish/distinguishes)
6. Objects ________________ light into the human eye. (reflects/reflect)

Directions: Write the correct present-tense form of each verb in ( ) on the line.

________________ 7. Warm colors (include) red, orange, and yellow.

________________ 8. Most often, a rainbow (appear) after rain has fallen.

________________ 9. My younger brother (splash) in puddles after storms.

________________ 10. He also (look) up at rainbows and (smile).

________________ 11. Then our grandparents (photograph) us.

Directions: Complete the sentences. Include a verb in the present tense that agrees with each subject.

12. Sometimes a rainbow ______________________________.
13. The paint on the wall ______________________________.
14. Some modern cameras ______________________________.
15. The school colors ______________________________.
16. A large color photograph ______________________________.
17. The trees in summer ______________________________.

Write a Poem

On a separate sheet of paper, write a poem about a beautiful sunset or autumn landscape. Make sure your verbs agree with your subjects.

Notes for Home: Your child used verbs in sentences to make subjects and verbs agree. ***Home Activity:*** Say a verb to your child *(run, sing, play)* and have him or her use the verb in sentences with a singular subject and a plural subject. Switch roles.

Name ________________________________

Predicates

REVIEW

Directions: Underline the complete predicate in each sentence. Then circle the simple predicate. (There may be more than one simple predicate in a sentence.)

1. Susan B. Anthony fought for women's rights for 55 years.
2. As a young woman, she worked in the anti-slavery movement.
3. Her efforts helped the passage of the 14th Amendment to the Constitution.
4. That amendment forbade slavery and made citizens of all slaves.
5. At the time, however, women possessed very few rights.
6. Susan B. Anthony saw the similarity between the issues of women's rights and slavery.
7. She met Elizabeth Stanton in 1851 and planned a course of action.
8. They created the National Women's Suffrage Association in 1869.
9. Both women campaigned throughout the country and lobbied members of Congress to allow women to vote.
10. The 19th Amendment to the Constitution passed in Congress 14 years after Susan B. Anthony's death.

Directions: Add a predicate to each subject to form a sentence. Write the complete sentence on the line.

11. Women in the past ____________.

____

12. Women today ____________.

____

13. Women in the future ____________.

____

14. Laws ____________.

____

15. My mother ____________.

____

Notes for Home: Your child identified simple and complete predicates. ***Home Activity:*** To reinforce this lesson, have your child identify the simple predicates in the five sentences he or she wrote above.

Name ______________________________

Verbs

A **verb** is the main word in the predicate of a sentence. An **action verb** tells what action the subject performs. Sometimes the action takes place in someone's mind.

Ruri <u>worked</u> hard for many years.
She <u>wanted</u> to save as much money as she could.

A **linking verb** links, or joins, the subject with a word or group of words in the predicate that tells something about the subject, such as what the subject is or how the subject feels.

Linking verbs are either forms of *be,* such as *am, is, are, was,* and *were,* or verbs like *feel, seem,* and *become.*

Ruri's new restaurant <u>is</u> great.
She <u>seems</u> very happy about the results of her work.

Directions: Underline the action verb in each sentence.

1. Ruri designed the entire restaurant.
2. She chose the furniture and the lighting.
3. Sometimes Ruri worried about her goals.
4. Often, she asked her sister for advice.
5. Ruri trusts her sister more than anyone else.
6. Ruri and her sister planned the menus for the restaurant.
7. They wanted a mix of different types of foods.
8. Ruri always uses fresh produce and meats.
9. She buys them from the local farmers.
10. Her customers appreciate all of Ruri's efforts.

Directions: Underline the linking verb in each sentence.

11. Ruri's business certainly seems successful.
12. The restaurant is almost always full.
13. I am a regular customer at the restaurant.
14. The servers are polite and helpful.
15. Diners always feel good at Ruri's.

Notes for Home: Your child identified action verbs, such as *run* or *think,* and linking verbs, such as *was* or *feel.* ***Home Activity:*** Have your child write three sentences that describe things he or she did in school. Help your child identify each action verb or linking verb.

Name ______________________________

Verbs

Directions: Underline the verb in each sentence. Write **A** if the verb is an action verb. Write **L** if it is a linking verb.

__________ **1.** Ken and Liam picked a project for the school fair.

__________ **2.** They made a short videotape about the history of the school.

__________ **3.** The two friends interviewed many former teachers and students.

__________ **4.** Some people felt shy about talking on camera.

__________ **5.** Ken and Liam also found old photographs and pictures of the school.

__________ **6.** The boys worked on the videotape for six weeks.

__________ **7.** Despite the difficulties, the final, edited tape was wonderful.

Directions: For each word in the box, write a sentence that tells about a person or a group of people you admire.

admire	excels	encourages

8. ______________________________

____

9. ______________________________

____

10. ______________________________

____

Write a Letter

On a separate sheet of paper, write a letter telling a friend about a task that was difficult. Include details to explain why the task was hard and how you completed it. When you are finished, underline all action verbs and circle all linking verbs.

Notes for Home: Your child identified action verbs, such as *run* or *think,* and linking verbs, such as *was* or *feel.* ***Home Activity:*** Have your child write three sentences that describe a favorite book. Help your child identify the action verbs or linking verbs in each sentence.

Name ______________________

Verbs

Read each sentence. The complete predicate is underlined. Write each simple predicate.

1. A bird is a pretty creature. ________
2. Plovers are one kind of bird. ________
3. They eat insects and worms. ________

An **action verb** expresses action the subject performs. Linking verbs, such as **is, was, being, am, are, were,** and **been,** join the subject to a word or group of words in the predicate.

Directions: Write the verb in each sentence on the line.

1. All plovers migrate from place to place. ________
2. They run with energy. ________
3. They build nests in a safe spot on the ground. ________
4. Some make their homes along the seashore. ________
5. Some live in fields or on plains. ________
6. The golden plover migrates long distances. ________
7. It breeds in Arctic regions. ________
8. Some plovers stay in Florida during winter months. ________
9. The bird flies about 2,400 miles over open ocean. ________
10. We have a picture of a plover in our living room. ________
11. They are small birds with long legs. ________

Directions: Circle the verb in each sentence. Write **action** or **linking** on the line.

12. The killdeer is a type of plover. ________
13. People recognize its shrill cry of "kill-deer." ________
14. Two black bands mark its white breast. ________
15. The feathers on its back are grayish-brown. ________
16. The female lays four black-spotted eggs. ________

Notes for Home: Your child identified action verbs and linking verbs in sentences. ***Home Activity:*** Have your child use this page to explain the differences between action and linking verbs. Ask him or her to provide other examples of action and linking verbs in sentences.

Name ______________________________

Verbs

Directions: Underline the verb in each sentence. Write each one. Then write **A** if it is an action verb or **L** if it is a linking verb.

1. Ants live together in large communities. ____________
2. The queen ant lays eggs. ____________
3. Worker ants feed the young. ____________
4. The nests contain many chambers. ____________
5. Many ant homes are in mounds of earth. ____________
6. Ants develop in several stages. ____________
7. Tiny white eggs hatch in a few weeks. ____________
8. Some ants live for several years. ____________
9. A few reach the age of fifteen years. ____________
10. Carpenter ants were destructive to human homes. ____________
11. One kind of hunter ant destroys harmful pests. ____________
12. All ants belong to the same family of insects. ____________

Directions: Circle the verb in each sentence. Write **action** or **linking** on the line.

13. Ants store food in their nest. ____________
14. Some kinds of ants eat grass seed. ____________
15. Another gathers grain for food. ____________
16. Another insect is an important partner of ants. ____________
17. This insect produces a sweet honeydew. ____________
18. This fluid nourishes the ants. ____________
19. Some ants are dormant in the winter. ____________
20. Other kinds of ants destroy harmful pests. ____________

Write a Funny Song

On a separate sheet of paper, write a funny song about your least favorite insect. Use precise and colorful verbs to describe the insect's behavior.

Notes for Home: Your child identified action and linking verbs in sentences. ***Home Activity:*** Say a sentence with two verbs. Have your child say another sentence, using one of those verbs and another of his or her choosing. Continue with other verbs.

Name ____________________

REVIEW

Verbs

Directions: Circle the verb in each sentence. Write **A** if the verb is an action verb. Write **L** if the verb is a linking verb. Remember, an **action verb** tells what action the subject performs. Sometimes the action takes place in someone's mind. A **linking verb** links, or joins, the subject with a word or group of words in the predicate that tells something about the subject, such as what the subject is or how the subject feels.

______ **1.** My class at school earned $200 last year.

______ **2.** Everyone worked for neighbors or relatives.

______ **3.** Some of the work was very hard.

______ **4.** José raked huge piles of leaves.

______ **5.** His hands looked sore the next day.

______ **6.** I cleaned my grandmother's garbage cans.

______ **7.** Whew! They were smelly!

______ **8.** I held my nose the whole time.

______ **9.** Others recycled newspapers and cans.

______ **10.** Everyone felt good at the end of the day.

Directions: Use each verb in a sentence. Write the sentence on the line.

11. *looked* as an action verb

____

12. *looked* as a linking verb

____

13. *felt* as an action verb

____

14. *felt* as a linking verb

____

15. *sounded* as a linking verb

____

Notes for Home: Your child identified action and linking verbs. ***Home Activity:*** Ask your child to find a paragraph that he or she has written. Go through the paragraph together, replacing any dull, overused verbs, such as *say, go,* and *do,* with more interesting verbs.

Name ______________________________

Verb Tenses: Present, Past, and Future

A verb in the **present tense** shows action that is happening now. Many present-tense verbs that work with singular subjects end in **-s** or **-es.**

Lucas works every Saturday with me. He misses his former free time, however.

Present-tense verbs that work with plural subjects do not usually add **-s** or **-es.**

Lucas and I work for Mr. Polito.

A verb in the **past tense** shows action that has already happened. Many verbs in the past tense end with **-ed.** Those that do not end with **-ed** are called **irregular verbs.** Since they do not follow a regular pattern of verb endings, you need to remember the past-tense forms.

Regular verb: Lucas and I worked for Mr. Polito.
Irregular verb: We went to his house every day for three weeks.

A verb in the **future tense** shows action that will happen. Verbs in the future tense include the helping verb *will.*

Next week, we will paint Mr. Polito's fence. Light gray paint will look best.

Directions: Write **present, past,** or **future** to tell the tense of each underlined verb.

______________ **1.** Mr. Polito hired us to work in his yard.

______________ **2.** Sometimes, things are harder than they look.

______________ **3.** Our lawnmower broke, and we had to find another.

______________ **4.** We always prepare fully for each job.

______________ **5.** We know that, sometimes, accidents will happen.

______________ **6.** Recently, we painted Mrs. Warner's shed.

______________ **7.** Now, the shed looks brand new.

______________ **8.** For a while, we thought we would never finish.

______________ **9.** Mrs. Warner's dog often barks when strangers are in the yard.

______________ **10.** That dog will bother you whenever you want to do something.

Notes for Home: Your child identified whether a verb was in the present, past, or future tense. ***Home Activity:*** Choose a verb, such as *wash* or *ride*. Have your child use the verb in three sentences, using a different tense for each sentence.

Name ______________________________

Verb Tenses: Present, Past, and Future

Directions: Circle the correct tense of the verb in ( ). Write **present, past,** or **future** to name the tense you chose.

______________ **1.** My brother (laughed/will laugh) when he finds out about my plans.

______________ **2.** He thinks that I (will be/am) a big dreamer.

______________ **3.** He (tells/told) me so just last week.

______________ **4.** Next month, I (will try/tried) to join the school's swimming team.

______________ **5.** I (learned/will learn) how to swim only last year.

______________ **6.** Nevertheless, I think I (will succeed/succeeds).

______________ **7.** Now, I (practice/practiced) every afternoon.

______________ **8.** Yesterday, I (swam/swim) for more than an hour.

______________ **9.** My brother (will wonder/wondered) why I have spent so much time at the pool.

______________ **10.** He often (will say/says) that I am like a fish.

______________ **11.** Swimming (does/did) a person's whole body a great deal of good.

______________ **12.** As I get better, I (will develop/developed) stronger muscles.

______________ **13.** This sport (helps/help) me build a swimmer's heart and lungs.

______________ **14.** Somehow, the Australian crawl never (tired/will tire) me when I was doing laps.

______________ **15.** The swim coach (watched/will watch) the rhythm of my strokes as I swim.

Write a Paragraph

Think of something that you dream of doing, such as being a veterinarian or traveling around the world. On a separate sheet of paper, write a paragraph about your dream. As you write, remember to use the correct tense for each verb.

Notes for Home: Your child chose verbs in the past, present, and future tenses to complete sentences. ***Home Activity:*** Invite your child to write sentences about something that happened yesterday and something that will happen tomorrow.

Name ______________________________

RETEACHING

Verb Tenses: Present, Past, and Future

Write **present, past,** or **future** to show when each event happens.

1. In 1911, Roald Amundsen reached the South Pole. ______________________
2. He lived in Antarctica for a year. ______________________
3. Now we learn about his struggles. ______________________
4. We give him credit for his achievements. ______________________
5. Next week Luisa will do a report about him. ______________________
6. Someday I will read Amundsen's autobiography. ______________________

The **tense** of a verb shows when the action happens. The past-tense form of most verbs ends in **-ed.** The future tense is usually formed with the helping verb **will**.

Directions: Underline the verb in each sentence below. On the line, write **present, past,** or **future** to show the tense of the verb.

1. I will finish this book about Amundsen tomorrow. ______________
2. Amundsen's books about his adventures interest me. ______________
3. They tell the story of his explorations. ______________
4. He studied science for many years. ______________
5. From 1903 to 1906 he completed his first important expedition. ______________
6. We know of his voyage through the Northwest Passage. ______________
7. You will learn about his stay in Antarctica. ______________
8. He lived there in the bitter cold for a year. ______________
9. He finally reached the South Pole. ______________
10. His endurance of physical hardships still amazes us. ______________
11. Our class will learn about his flight over the North Pole. ______________
12. He traveled seventy hours in an airship. ______________
13. In 1928, Amundsen died during a rescue mission. ______________
14. Our class will read about his death at sea. ______________
15. I enjoy stories about heroic lives. ______________

Notes for Home: Your child identified tenses of verbs in sentences. ***Home Activity:*** Have your child choose some sentences in a favorite story and identify the tense of each verb. Then have him or her say new sentences with the verbs in different tenses.

More Verb Tenses: Perfect and Progressive Tenses

The **present perfect tense** describes an action that began in the past and is completed in the present. It is formed by adding **has** or **have** to the past participle. The **past participle** of any regular verb is formed by adding **-ed** to the present tense.

The track-and-field committee has elected a new chairperson.

The **past perfect tense** describes an action begun at one point in the past and completed at another point in the past. It is formed by adding **had** to the past participle.

Until last week, Denise had attended all the committee meetings.

The **future perfect tense** describes an action to be completed at a particular time in the future. It is formed by adding **will have** to the past participle.

By next week, the committee will have created a new track schedule.

To describe an action that is ongoing, or in progress, you can use the **progressive** form of a tense. Each progressive form includes the **present participle,** the **-ing** form, of the main verb.

Roland is practicing every day. (present progressive)

Sally was recovering from a knee injury. (past progressive)

Directions: Use the correct form of the verb in ( ) to complete each sentence. Use the verb in the tense named in ( ). Write the verb on the line to the left.

______________ **1.** By last week, Tina _____ three different field events. (enter—past perfect)

______________ **2.** Tyrell _____ to improve his time in the 100-yard dash. (try—past progressive)

______________ **3.** The school _____ the new indoor track. (finish—past perfect)

______________ **4.** Our team _____ in five meets. (compete—present perfect)

______________ **5.** We _____ in twenty meets by the time the season ends. (compete—future perfect)

______________ **6.** We _____ money for new uniforms. (raise—present progressive)

______________ **7.** The fan club _____ two hundred dollars. (donate—past perfect)

______________ **8.** Soon we _____ all the money we need. (raise—future perfect)

______________ **9.** Our coach _____ a banquet. (plan—present progressive)

______________ **10.** I _____ to be chosen as the most improved athlete. (hope—present progressive)

Notes for Home: Your child wrote verbs in the perfect and progressive tenses. ***Home Activity:*** Have your child use the present progressive tense to describe actions happening now.

Name ______________________________

More Verb Tenses: Perfect and Progressive Tenses

Directions: Use the correct form of the verb in ( ) to complete each sentence. Use the verb in the tense named in ( ). Write the verb on the line to the left.

______________ **1.** My friends and I _____ a new outdoor track for a long time. (want—present perfect)

______________ **2.** We _____ hundreds of signatures for our petitions. (collect—present perfect)

______________ **3.** We _____ everything we can to get this track built. (do—present progressive)

______________ **4.** By next year, we hope the school _____ to build the track. (agree—future perfect)

______________ **5.** Until last month, the school board _____ our petitions and letters. (ignore—past perfect)

______________ **6.** Our classmates _____ us advice and support. (give—past progressive)

______________ **7.** In the past month, other board members _____ to consider our idea. (start—past perfect)

______________ **8.** Our group _____ how to present our ideas more clearly. (learn—present progressive)

______________ **9.** Surely, by the next board meeting, we _____ five other members. (convince—future perfect)

______________ **10.** We _____ everyone why our plan makes sense. (show—present progressive)

Write a Short Story

On a separate sheet of paper, write a story that shares a lesson that you learned about someone or something. When you have finished, identify the tenses of the verbs you used.

Notes for Home: Your child wrote verbs in perfect and progressive tenses. ***Home Activity:*** Have your child use the past perfect tense to describe a past action. *(I had studied for that test for weeks!)*

Name ______________________________

More Verb Tenses: Perfect and Progressive Tenses

RETEACHING

Underline the correct verb form in ( ) that best completes each sentence.

1. After a week of discussion, we (decide/have decided) not to go. **(present perfect)**
2. Until yesterday, Dan (ran/had run) two miles every day. **(past perfect)**
3. By 3:30, we (have/will have) completed the test. **(future perfect)**
4. Our book club (reading/is reading) every day. **(present progressive)**
5. June (eats/was eating) when her mother came home. **(past progressive)**

The **present perfect tense** describes an action that began in the past and ends in the present. It is formed by adding **has** or **have** to the **past participle** (the **-ed** form) of a regular verb. The **past perfect tense** describes an action that began and ended in the past. It is formed by adding **had** to the past participle. The **future perfect tense** describes an action that will be completed in the future. It is formed by adding **will have** to the past participle. Use a **progressive** form of a tense to describe an action that is in progress. This form includes the **present participle** (the **-ing** form) of the main verb.

Directions: Use the correct form of the verb in ( ) to complete each sentence. Use the verb in the tense named in ( ). Write the verb on the line.

______________________ 1. We _____ aluminum cans last month. (collect—past perfect)

______________________ 2. We _____ them to the supermarket in baskets. (carry—past perfect)

______________________ 3. The clerk _____ them carefully. (count—past perfect)

______________________ 4. We _____ our quota by tomorrow. (fill—future perfect)

______________________ 5. My brother and I _____ money to buy CDs. (save—present progressive)

______________________ 6. He _____ it all on gum and candy. (spend—past progressive)

______________________ 7. I told him that if we _____ to have a better CD collection, we needed to budget our money. (go—past progressive)

______________________ 8. So far, we _____ enough money to buy one and a half CDs. (save—present perfect)

______________________ 9. After tomorrow we _____ the right amount for two CDs. (earn—future perfect)

Notes for Home: Your child used progressive and perfect forms of verb tenses to complete sentences. ***Home Activity:*** Together, look at an article in a newspaper and have your child identify examples of sentences with progressive and perfect forms of verb tenses.

Name ______________________________

More Verb Tenses: Perfect and Progressive Tenses

Directions: Read each sentence. Identify the tense of each underlined verb. Write the name of the tense on the line.

______________ 1. I have located some interesting photographs.

______________ 2. My grandmother had stored them in the attic.

______________ 3. I was looking for an old stuffed animal when I came across them.

______________ 4. Tonight she has shared them with me.

______________ 5. By tomorrow I will have recorded much information.

______________ 6. My great-grandfather had performed in many concerts.

______________ 7. He had achieved fame as a pianist.

______________ 8. My great-grandmother had played the violin with him.

______________ 9. My grandmother was saving pictures of them.

______________ 10. We will have mounted them in a book by next week.

______________ 11. We have discovered recordings of their performances.

______________ 12. In a year we will have donated them to the library.

______________ 13. The library is collecting old photos and recordings for a new exhibit about our town's history.

______________ 14. One librarian was asking for photos of people and the places they lived.

______________ 15. My great-grandmother is smiling in many of the photographs.

Directions: Write a sentence with the verb and tense named in ( ). Write each new sentence on the line.

16. (understand—past progressive)

____

17. (try—present progressive)

____

18. (find—past perfect)

____

Notes for Home: Your child identified tenses of verbs and wrote sentences using verbs in perfect and progressive tenses. ***Home Activity:*** Together, list verbs related to your child's hobby or special skill. Have your child write sentences, using those verbs in perfect and progressive tenses.

Using Correct Verb Tenses

REVIEW

Directions: Read each sentence. Circle the correct form of the verb in ( ) to best complete each sentence.

1. Last year the mayor (invites/invited) a minor league team to our city.
2. No one (attended/had attended) a minor league game before.
3. My family (likes/is liking) baseball very much.
4. For years we (follow/had followed) teams like the Yankees and the Bluejays.
5. We (will go/went) to the opening game last night.
6. We saw that everyone (is playing/was playing) as hard as possible.
7. At the end, the crowd yelled and (cheers/cheered).
8. We were excited when our team (won/wins) 7–4.
9. Now our town (bragged/is bragging) proudly about the Santon Seagulls.
10. Next week we (will get/were getting) season tickets to the games of this minor league team.

Directions: Add a word or words to each verb to form a sentence. Write the complete sentence on the line.

11. wish

____

12. am wishing

____

13. wished

____

14. have wished

____

15. will wish

____

Notes for Home: Your child practiced using the correct tenses of verbs. ***Home Activity:*** Extend the second part of this activity by having your child create sentences for the following verb tenses: *ask, am asking, asked,* and *had asked.*

Name ______________________________

Irregular Verbs

Regular verbs are verbs that have the same spelling in the past and past participle forms. The **past form** of **regular verbs** is formed by adding **-ed** to the present tense. The **past participle** form of regular verbs is also formed by adding **-ed** to the present tense. It uses a helping verb such as *has* or *have.*

Present: We watch my little brother play baseball.

Past: We watched my little brother play baseball.

Past Participle: We have watched my little brother play baseball many times.

Irregular verbs, however, have different spellings for the past and past participle forms.

Present: He throws the runner out at first base.

Past: He threw the runner out at first base.

Past Participle: This is the third time he has thrown the runner out at first base.

Directions: Write **regular** or **irregular** to describe each underlined verb.

______________________ **1.** The Glenview Gators were one of the best teams in the league.

______________________ **2.** They had a great pitcher.

______________________ **3.** They usually scored at least seven runs a game.

______________________ **4.** They just won against the Janesville Giants 8–2.

______________________ **5.** I hoped our team would clobber them tonight.

Directions: Use a form of the verb shown in ( ) to best complete each sentence. Write the verb on the line.

______________________ **6.** Although we lost, our team (play) well against the tough Gators.

______________________ **7.** Our star player had (steal) home, and the score was tied.

______________________ **8.** Then, our pitcher (strike) out the lead batter.

______________________ **9.** I (catch) a long fly ball to center field to make it two outs.

______________________ **10.** But then the Mighty Margoles hit a grand slam, and our team had (lose) again.

Notes for Home: Your child identified regular and irregular verbs and wrote the past and past participle forms of verbs. ***Home Activity:*** Have your child describe three things he or she did today. For each sentence, ask him or her whether the verbs are regular or irregular.

Name ______________________________

Irregular Verbs

Directions: Write **regular** or **irregular** to describe each underlined verb.

__________ **1.** Lucy has joined the girls' softball team.

__________ **2.** She wanted to be a pitcher, but they made her a catcher instead.

__________ **3.** She has taken a lot of teasing for the bulky pads she wears.

__________ **4.** In the last game, she ran into the dugout to catch a foul ball.

__________ **5.** She tries harder than any player I have seen.

Directions: Write the correct form for each irregular verb below.

Present	Past	Past Participle
begin	**6.** __________	**7.** has/have __________
come	**8.** __________	**9.** has/have __________
eat	**10.** __________	**11.** has/have __________
fall	**12.** __________	**13.** has/have __________
ring	**14.** __________	**15.** has/have __________
bring	**16.** __________	**17.** has/have __________
swim	**18.** __________	**19.** has/have __________
say	**20.** __________	**21.** has/have __________
know	**22.** __________	**23.** has/have __________
drive	**24.** __________	**25.** has/have __________

Write a Diary Entry

On a separate sheet of paper, write a diary entry about an event that turned out differently than you had expected. The event can be either real or made up. Underline the regular verbs and circle the irregular verbs. Be careful to write the correct forms of irregular verbs.

Notes for Home: Your child identified regular verbs and irregular verbs. ***Home Activity:*** Choose several irregular verbs (such as *swing, give,* and *grow*). Have your child use each verb in a sentence that describes an action that took place in the past.

Name ______________________________________

RETEACHING

Irregular Verbs

Find the verbs in these sentences. Write them in the blanks. Be sure to include any helping verbs.

1. Luis and Liam swim this week. ______________________ (present)
2. They swam last week too. ______________________ (past)
3. The team has swum every day this month. ______________ (past participle)

The past and past participle forms of **irregular verbs** are not made by adding **-ed.** Instead, the spelling of each verb changes to make each form.

Directions: Underline the irregular verb in each sentence. Write **past** or **past participle** to tell which verb form is used.

1. Our swim team has begun regular practices. ________________
2. Some of us had swum on the team before this year. ________________
3. The coach wrote our practice schedule on a chart. ________________
4. She had given a lot of thought to the schedule. ________________
5. Then we went to the deep end of the pool. ________________
6. We have grown accustomed to the routine. ________________
7. We knew it was for our own good. ________________

Directions: Write the correct verb form in ( ) to complete each sentence.

8. The coach ________________ her whistle. (blew/blown)
9. Two of the boys had ________________ five laps. (swam/swum)
10. They had ________________ enough backstroke laps. (did/done)
11. She ________________ the boys three minutes to rest. (gave/given)
12. They ________________ towels around their shoulders. (threw/thrown)
13. The coach had ________________ down their times. (wrote/written)
14. I ________________ some milk after practice. (drank/drunk)
15. We had ________________ a good breakfast at sunrise. (ate/eaten)

Notes for Home: Your child identified irregular verbs in past and past participle forms. ***Home Activity:*** Have your child read a page from "Casey at the Bat" and identify irregular verbs in past participle forms.

Name ____________________

Irregular Verbs

Directions: Write the correct verb form as indicated in ( ).

1. drink (past participle) has ________ **2.** blow (past participle) has ________

3. sing (past) ________ **4.** grow (past) ________

5. eat (past) ________ **6.** go (past participle) has ________

7. throw (past participle) has ________ **8.** take (past participle) has ________

Directions: Complete each sentence by writing the past or past participle form of the verb in ( ).

9. Our visit to the state fair ________ just before lunch. (begin)

10. Everyone ________ the food at the fair was great. (know)

11. Before long we had ________ several ears of roasted corn. (eat)

12. Four-year-old Jacob ________ to find Belgian waffles. (go)

13. He had ________ very fond of these giant pastries. (grow)

14. He ________ half of his snack to his cousin Rachel. (give)

Directions: Complete each sentence with a verb form that makes sense. Write on the line the past or past participle form of one of the verbs in the box.

take	sing	give	blow	eat	fly

15. After lunch a whistle ________ to start the steer-judging competition.

16. The judges had ________ all the prizes.

17. It ________ much more time to judge the hogs and milk cows.

18. Later a famous entertainer ________ popular songs in the music tent.

19. He had ________ from Hollywood to the fairgrounds just for the day.

20. By evening Jacob had ________ two more Belgian waffles.

Write a Paragraph

On a separate sheet of paper, write a paragraph about a fair or a carnival. Use irregular verbs in some of your sentences.

Notes for Home: Your child wrote irregular verbs in past-tense and past participle forms. ***Home Activity:*** Discuss with your child what the two of you did today. Have your child give a hand signal every time one of you uses an irregular verb.

Name ______________________________

Subject-Verb Agreement

REVIEW

Directions: Circle the verb in ( ) that agrees with the subject in each sentence.

1. (Does/Do) the students in your class know the names of all the planets?
2. Mercury (is/are) the closest planet to the Sun.
3. This small planet (orbits/orbit) the Sun every 88 days.
4. The thick clouds around Venus (makes/make) the astronomer's job very difficult.
5. Mars, more than the other planets, (has/have) been the subject of many scary movies about space creatures.
6. An asteroid belt (exists/exist) between Mars and Jupiter.
7. Even amateur astronomers (enjoys/enjoy) the rings around Saturn.
8. A recent discovery by powerful telescopes (shows/show) rings around Jupiter too.
9. Jupiter, of course, (is/are) the largest planet.
10. Perhaps other planets beyond Pluto (awaits/await) our discovery.

Directions: Match each subject with a verb in the box. Then write a sentence that includes both of them.

launches	rotates	searches	shines	watches
launch	rotate	search	shine	watch

11. An astronomer ____________________.

____

12. Mission control ____________________.

____

13. Earth ____________________.

____

14. Space probes ____________________.

____

15. Stars ____________________.

____

Notes for Home: Your child identified verbs that agree with their subjects. ***Home Activity:*** Together, listen to stories on tape or a program on television. Repeat sentences aloud and discuss whether the subject-verb agreement is correct.

Name ______________________________________

Direct and Indirect Objects and Subject Complements

A **direct object** is a noun or pronoun that follows an action verb and tells who or what receives the action of the verb.

I watched a long movie on TV last night.

The views of Earth from outer space surprised me.

An **indirect object** comes after an action verb. It names the person to whom or for whom the action is done. However, the words *to* or *for* are not used before an indirect object.

I wrote Maria a note about the movie.

In this sentence, *Maria* is the indirect object of *wrote*. The word *note* is the direct object.

A **predicate noun** follows a linking verb and tells who or what the subject is.

Maria is a former neighbor of mine.

A **predicate adjective** follows a linking verb and describes the subject.

Maria has become enthusiastic about flying.

Directions: Underline each direct object once and each indirect object twice. Hint: Not every sentence has an indirect object.

1. I discovered an article about the Wright brothers.
2. The article gave me ideas about working on inventions.
3. I wrote an essay about their experiments with a glider.
4. My cousin Maxine read the paper carefully.
5. Maxine gave me her reactions in writing.

Directions: Write **PN** if the underlined word is a predicate noun. Write **PA** if it is a predicate adjective.

______________ 6. From glider flight to space flight, the progress has been amazing.

______________ 7. I felt astonished to learn that 1903 was the date of the first engine-powered flight.

______________ 8. The young Wright brothers were experienced mechanics.

______________ 9. Their patience with repeated failures seems remarkable.

______________ 10. Naturally, these two men became celebrities.

Notes for Home: Your child identified direct and indirect objects, as well as predicate nouns and adjectives. ***Home Activity:*** Use the examples and definitions above to help your child write additional examples.

Name ______________________________

Direct and Indirect Objects and Subject Complements

Directions: Write **DO** if the underlined word is a direct object. Write **IO** if it is an indirect object.

__________ **1.** Julia sent her <u>relatives</u> some letters.

__________ **2.** She wanted true <u>stories</u> about successful work experiences.

__________ **3.** Some of the relatives wrote <u>notes</u> to Julia.

__________ **4.** Uncle Bob mailed <u>her</u> a tape instead.

__________ **5.** Bob told Julia a fascinating <u>story</u> about his work with NASA's space exploration.

__________ **6.** Bob gave his <u>niece</u> many suggestions for her own life.

__________ **7.** Then he assigned <u>her</u> a little exercise.

__________ **8.** Julia described the <u>exercise</u> to her mother.

__________ **9.** "He has sent <u>you</u> many sensible ideas," Julia's mother said.

__________ **10.** Julia shared her mother's <u>comment</u> with her uncle.

Directions: Circle the linking verb in each sentence. Remember to circle any helping verbs. Then underline the sentence part named in ( ).

11. Julia clearly felt interested in her relatives' ideas. (predicate adjective)

12. Sometimes relatives are the best advisers. (predicate noun)

13. Her uncle certainly seems kind. (predicate adjective)

14. He also has been generous with his time. (predicate adjective)

15. Uncle Bob's story will become a part of the family history. (predicate noun)

Write a Narrative Paragraph

On a separate sheet of paper, write a narrative paragraph (a very short story) about a time when you helped someone or someone helped you. Try to include one or more direct objects, indirect objects, predicate nouns, and predicate adjectives. List the direct and indirect objects and the predicate nouns and adjectives you used below your paragraph.

Notes for Home: Your child identified direct objects (Mary sent a *<u>card</u>*) and indirect objects *(Mary sent <u>her</u> a card)*, as well as predicate nouns and adjectives. ***Home Activity:*** Have your child write a sentence that includes a direct object and an indirect object.

Name ______________________________

RETEACHING

Direct and Indirect Objects and Subject Complements

Underline the direct object in each sentence. Circle each indirect object.

1. Gloria gave me a wonderful birthday present.
2. I sent her a thank-you note yesterday.

Underline the predicate noun. Circle the predicate adjective.

3. Gloria is thoughtful about other people.
4. She became an artist after several years of work.

A **direct object** is the noun or noun phrase that follows an action verb and tells who or what receives the action of the verb. An **indirect object** is the noun or noun phrase that often directly follows an action verb and names the person to whom or for whom the action is done. A **predicate noun** follows a linking verb and tells who or what the subject is. A **predicate adjective** also follows a linking verb, and it describes the subject.

Directions: Underline each direct object once and each indirect object twice. Not every sentence will have both.

1. My friends celebrated my birthday early this year.
2. Each of them brought me a silly gift.
3. Mark gave me ten soda straws in a used milk carton.
4. Yoshi sang us a song backwards.
5. My father cooked chicken.
6. I gave each of my friends a big hug.

Directions: Write whether each underlined word is a **predicate noun** or a **predicate adjective.**

______________________ 7. Now the sun is low in the sky.

______________________ 8. I am a photographer in the city.

______________________ 9. Some people here are very busy.

______________________ 10. Pushing heavy bricks seems easy for that worker.

______________________ 11. The afternoon seemed long and hot.

Notes for Home: Your child identified direct and indirect objects and predicate nouns and adjectives. ***Home Activity:*** Have your child write two questions containing direct and indirect objects. Answer the questions, using direct and indirect objects. Have your child check your work.

Name ______________________________

Direct and Indirect Objects and Subject Complements

Directions: Write **DO** if the underlined word is a direct object. Write **IO** if it is an indirect object.

______________ **1.** When my Aunt Sarah moved to Germany, she left us many things.

______________ **2.** One thing she gave us was her collection of ukuleles.

______________ **3.** Aunt Sarah collected musical instruments from different countries.

______________ **4.** She told my cousins stories about how and where the instruments were made.

______________ **5.** Some villagers in a little town in Ireland had made some drums she had.

______________ **6.** Aunt Sarah gave me her drums because she knew I liked to play them when I visited her.

______________ **7.** My brother wanted her many books about instruments made out of gourds.

______________ **8.** Now that she has left, we have sent her thank-you cards for all the gifts she gave us.

______________ **9.** In my card I told her what I did with the gifts.

______________ **10.** My brother and I miss the stories she told us.

Directions: Circle the linking verb in each sentence. Then underline each predicate adjective once and each predicate noun twice. Not every sentence will have both a predicate adjective and a predicate noun.

11. "Beth is my aunt," said my friend.

12. "I am curious about her job as a calligrapher. How should I ask her my questions?"

13. "Writing a letter seems smart," I told him.

14. "You are right!" he said.

15. Her response was very interesting.

16. She had been a calligrapher a long time ago.

17. Her entire letter was beautiful.

Notes for Home: Your child identified direct and indirect objects and predicate nouns and adjectives in sentences. ***Home Activity:*** Have your child identify in a favorite story two sentences with direct and indirect objects. Then have him or her use the direct and indirect objects in new sentences.

Name ______________________________

REVIEW

Complete Subjects

Directions: Underline the complete subject in each sentence.

1. The Abenaki people grew much of their own food.
2. One very important crop for their diet was corn.
3. A favorite Abenaki myth tells of the creation of this basic food.
4. A lonely man meets a mysterious woman one day.
5. Her long, flowing hair is remarkably fair and silky.
6. This lovely creature asks the man to follow her instructions carefully.
7. He first sets fire to a field.
8. The obedient man then pulls the woman gently over the ground by her long hair.
9. Her fair, silken hair will then reappear to him each year in the form of corn silks.
10. The gift of golden corn remains with the man and his people forever after.

Directions: Use each word as part of the complete subject in a sentence of your own. Your complete subject should have at least three words.

11. corn

____

____

12. myths

____

____

13. hair

____

____

14. crops

____

____

15. water

____

____

Notes for Home: Your child identified and wrote sentences with complete subjects—the part that tells whom or what the sentence is about. ***Home Activity:*** Look through a newspaper with your child. Identify the complete subjects of some sentences.

Name ______________________________

Adjectives

Adjectives modify, or tell more about, nouns or pronouns. Adjectives can tell what kind, which one, how many, or how much.

red sky (what kind) this village (which one) two miles (how many)

Most adjectives come before the nouns they modify. However, **predicate adjectives** follow linking verbs and modify a noun or pronoun in the subject.

Grandmother is very wise. She is also kind.

An adjective formed from a proper noun is called a **proper adjective.** Proper adjectives are capitalized.

European village South African music

Directions: Underline each adjective. Circle the noun it modifies.

1. Toni visited Grandmother's old village.
2. She saw ancient houses and uneven streets.
3. Greek villages seemed pleasant to her.
4. Young and old relatives crowded around her.
5. Toni's American clothes interested them.

Directions: Add adjectives to complete each sentence. Use the clues in ( ) to help. Write each adjective on the matching numbered line to the right.

6. _____ (how many) huge trees hung over the **7.** _____ (what kind) gate. From the gate, a **8.** _____ (what kind) path led to my uncle's **9.** _____ (what kind) garden. The garden had **10.** _____ (how many) different kinds of plants. **11.** _____ (which ones) plants all looked very **12.** _____ (what kind). I noticed that **13.** _____ (how many) plants had grown remarkably tall. Uncle Jim promised to teach me to raise plants as **14.** _____ (what kind) as his. I know I can learn **15.** _____ (which one) skill from my capable uncle.

6. ______________________

7. ______________________

8. ______________________

9. ______________________

10. ______________________

11. ______________________

12. ______________________

13. ______________________

14. ______________________

15. ______________________

Notes for Home: Your child identified and used adjectives—words that tell more about nouns and pronouns. ***Home Activity:*** Challenge your child to use as many adjectives as he or she can in describing someone or something. See if you can guess whom or what your child is describing.

Name ______________________________

Adjectives

Directions: Underline the adjective or adjectives in each sentence. Circle the noun each adjective modifies.

1. The Acoma people occupy an ancient pueblo on a mesa in the Southwest.
2. A mesa is flat at the top.
3. The Acoma still keep the old way of life.
4. They speak the first language of their ancestors.
5. They make beautiful pottery.

Directions: Choose an adjective from the box to complete each sentence. Write the adjective on the line to the left.

steep	young	traditional	hard	full
soft	high	Santa Fe	free	sagebrush

______________ **6.** The _____ children learn how to find clay in nearby canyons.

______________ **7.** They knead the stiff clay, and it becomes _____ enough to shape.

______________ **8.** The painted decorations for the pots are _____ designs that the children learned from their parents.

______________ **9.** Next, the children fire the painted pots, and the clay becomes _____.

______________ **10.** Then the Acoma sell the pots at a _____ market.

Write Instructions

Think about something a family member taught you how to do. You might have learned how to grow a garden, make pottery, or cook a traditional dish. Write a simple set of instructions that a friend could follow to make the same item. Use adjectives in your writing.

Notes for Home: Your child identified and used adjectives. ***Home Activity:*** Challenge your child to name something that you describe, using proper adjectives: *an American city* or *an Italian dish,* for example.

Name ______________________________

Adjectives

RETEACHING

Underline each adjective in the sentences.

1. We chose bright material for our new curtains.
2. I didn't want this day to end.
3. Toloma added six kiwis to her basket.
4. Rory the dog is very gentle.
5. We decided to try the Spanish rice.

Adjectives tell more about persons, places, or things that nouns name. Adjectives tell what kind, which one, or how many. Often adjectives appear before the nouns they tell more about. When an adjective appears in the predicate of the sentence, it follows a linking verb and is called a **predicate adjective.** A **proper adjective** is an adjective formed from a proper noun.

Directions: Underline each adjective. Then draw an arrow from each adjective to the noun it tells more about. Hint: There may be more than one adjective modifying the same noun.

1. This mountain had many glaciers.
2. Kim is a brave woman and a skillful climber.
3. She is strong too.
4. In the morning, she put on Norwegian athletic shoes.
5. The sky was pink at the start of the steep climb.
6. The crisp air chilled her.
7. Finally a red sun rose.
8. Kim saw purple flowers and blue dragonflies.
9. These lovely sights refreshed her.
10. Kim climbed over three huge boulders.
11. She rested beside a clear stream.
12. The icy water tasted sweet.

Notes for Home: Your child identified adjectives in sentences and the nouns that they tell about. ***Home Activity:*** Discuss with your child an important event at school. Encourage your child to use adjectives in the discussion.

Name ______________________________

Adjectives

Directions: Choose an adjective to sensibly complete each sentence. Write the adjective on the line.

1. ______________ week, my parents decided what our summer project would be.
2. They had been talking about it for ______________ weeks, and my sister and I had been guessing what our parents would choose.
3. Shaunita thought we would have to paint the ______________ garage because the paint was peeling off.
4. Then she mentioned that we might have to wash the ______________ doors in the dining room.
5. I was almost positive we would have to clean out the garage because it hadn't been cleaned in years, and it was ______________.
6. My brother guessed we would have to plant new bushes and shrubs in the ______________ yard.
7. At dinner one night, Mom and Dad announced their ______________ plan.
8. With help, we were going to refinish the ______________ deck behind our house.
9. My brother and sister and I would be in charge of choosing ______________ flowers and paint for the flower boxes and paint for the railings.
10. I chose ____________ flowers and ____________ and ____________ paint.
11. My brother didn't like that idea. He thought ______________ colors wouldn't match the house.
12. We finally agreed on ______________ color for both the flower boxes and the railings.

Directions: Circle each adjective. Underline the noun each adjective tells more about.

13. This summer we began our massive project.
14. My entire family put on their old, dirty clothes.
15. Then we called our helpful neighbors and held a meeting.
16. Mom explained the new project to all seven people.
17. She showed the neighbors the blue paint.
18. Then everyone began this exciting job.
19. We had to let the paint dry on the boxes before we could plant the English flowers.
20. It took us two weeks, but we finished the beautiful deck!

Notes for Home: Your child identified and wrote adjectives in sentences. ***Home Activity:*** Together, listen to a favorite song or instrumental piece. Talk about the music together. Encourage your child to use descriptive adjectives.

Name ____________________

REVIEW

Adjectives

Directions: Draw a line under each adjective. Circle the noun it modifies.

1. The enormous copper statue rises over the busy harbor of New York City.
2. The colossal work was a gift to the American people from France.
3. The huge stone pedestal, however, was built with American money.
4. President Cleveland dedicated the beautiful Statue of Liberty in 1886, and it soon became a powerful symbol of freedom.
5. In former years, when new immigrants arrived by ship, the towering statue provided the first sight of America.
6. Anxious newcomers hoping for improved lives in a free country were moved to tears when they saw the mighty lady.
7. In 1924, the famous and familiar statue was declared a national monument.
8. A steep spiral staircase inside the steel framework leads to the crown.
9. From the high crown, numerous visitors have looked out at the breathtaking view.
10. "Miss Liberty" is tall and proud, and she is known to the entire world.

Directions: Complete each sentence with an article or adjective from the box that tells how many or how much. Write the word on the line.

a *or* an	many	two	no	several

____________ **11.** Shana was one of _____ visitors to the Statue of Liberty that crisp fall day.

____________ **12.** She had come with _____ members of her family—her parents, brother, aunt, and uncle.

____________ **13.** They had had _____ food since breakfast, but they were too excited to eat.

____________ **14.** They had moved to America just _____ weeks ago.

____________ **15.** To Shana and her family, the huge statue was _____ amazing sight that they will never forget.

Notes for Home: Your child identified and used adjectives—words that tell more about nouns and pronouns. ***Home Activity:*** Write some of the adjectives on cards. Then have your child choose a card and use the adjective in a sentence.

Comparative and Superlative Adjectives

An adjective describes a person, a place, or a thing.

The **comparative form** of an adjective is used to compare two persons, places, or things. The word **than** sometimes signals this form.

These fireworks are brighter than last year's display.

The **superlative form** of an adjective is used to compare three or more persons, places, or things.

Next year's fireworks will be the brightest of all.

More and **most** are usually used in the comparative or superlative forms of adjectives.

Chili dogs are more delicious than plain hot dogs.
Dad makes the most delicious hot dogs on the grill.

Do not use **more** and **most** with adjectives ending in **-er** or **-est.**

Don't write: Mom's iced lemonade tastes more sweeter than my iced lemonade.
Write: Mom's iced lemonade tastes sweeter than my iced lemonade.

As shown below, the spelling of some adjectives changes in the comparative and superlative forms.

good, better, best	much, more, most
bad, worse, worst	little, less, least

Directions: Circle the correct form of the adjective in ( ) to complete each sentence.

1. To Clara, the Fourth of July was the (better/best) holiday of the year.
2. First, she would twirl her baton and march in the (bigger/biggest) parade in the entire state.
3. The band's uniforms were the (brighter/brightest) red she had ever seen.
4. The notes played by the flute section were (softer/softest) than those played by the trumpet section.
5. The float of the Statue of Liberty was the (larger/largest) of all.
6. Clara's family would always throw one of the (nicer/nicest) parties on the block.
7. Clara would help cook the (tastier/tastiest) hot dogs her friends had ever eaten.
8. In the evening, there would be a fireworks display with the (louder/loudest) noises ever!
9. The red starburst at the end was the (more brilliant/most brilliant) of all the fireworks.
10. Clara couldn't think of anything (better/best) than the Fourth of July.

Notes for Home: Your child identified and used comparative and superlative adjectives to compare people, places, and things. ***Home Activity:*** Challenge your child to think of a sentence with a comparative adjective. You, in turn, supply a sentence with a superlative adjective.

Name ______________________________

Comparative and Superlative Adjectives

Directions: Use the correct form of the adjective in ( ) to complete each sentence. Write the adjective on the line.

______________ **1.** Thanksgiving is the (great) holiday.

______________ **2.** My family gets together for a feast that's (good) than the one the Pilgrims had.

______________ **3.** Mom is (happy) of all, because my brother comes home from college.

______________ **4.** She always says he looks (tall) than he was when he left.

______________ **5.** We all laugh, but my brother laughs (loud) of all.

______________ **6.** He says he couldn't have grown any (big) than he was three months ago.

______________ **7.** We give thanks for the (good) life we have.

______________ **8.** Then we eat the (delicious) dinner of all—turkey, stuffing, potatoes, and squash.

______________ **9.** Mom's apple pie is (sweet) than her pumpkin pie.

______________ **10.** But I think pumpkin pie is the (good) dessert of all.

______________ **11.** After dinner, we watch the (exciting) football game that we can find on TV.

______________ **12.** My mom is (loyal) to the home team than my brother is.

______________ **13.** My brother thinks the team from his college town is (good) than ours.

______________ **14.** When it comes to sports, Mom and my brother have the (lively) discussions of anyone in our family.

______________ **15.** Mom says it's the (enjoyable) debate she has all year long.

Write a Description

Invent a new holiday. On a separate sheet of paper, give the holiday a name and describe what it celebrates. Then explain how people will observe the day. Will they have a parade? Will they prepare a special meal? Use comparative and superlative adjectives in your description.

Notes for Home: Your child wrote the comparative and superlative forms of adjectives. ***Home Activity:*** On small pieces of paper, write a variety of nouns. With your child, take turns choosing a noun and describing it with comparative and superlative forms of adjectives.

Name ______________________________

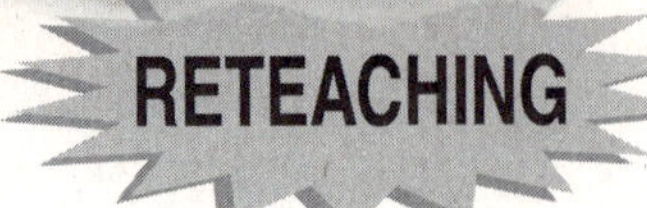

RETEACHING

Comparative and Superlative Adjectives

The chart below shows some forms of four adjectives. Fill in the missing adjectives in the chart.

	Adjective	Comparative Form	Superlative Form
1.	________	happier	happiest
2.	expensive	________	most expensive
3.	good	better	________
4.	bad	________	worst

Use the **comparative** form of an adjective to compare two items. Use the **superlative** form to compare three or more items. Most adjectives add **-er, -est, more,** or **most** to form the comparative and superlative forms. Some adjectives have special forms.

Directions: Write the correct adjective form in ( ) to complete each sentence.

1. Some people say the clipper ship was the ________ ship ever built. (more exciting/most exciting)
2. The vessel of Christopher Columbus's time was a ________ ship than the galley. (newer/newest)
3. Clipper ships were ________ than Columbus's ships. (larger/largest)
4. Of all sailing vessels, the clipper was the ________ ship. (faster/fastest)
5. The ________ clipper ship ever built was the Great Republic. (bigger/biggest)
6. Steamships have been ________ than sailing ships in recent times. (common/more common)
7. Steamships were ________ than sailing ships at maintaining a steady pace. (better/best)
8. These ships were the ________ ships of all time. (more powerful/most powerful)
9. Even today, however, many people find sailboats ________ than power boats. (enjoyable/more enjoyable)
10. The sailboat is ________ than the power boat. (most thrilling/more thrilling)

Notes for Home: Your child used comparative and superlative forms of adjectives in sentences. ***Home Activity:*** Take a walk with your child. Talk about what you see by saying sentences with adjectives in comparative and superlative forms.

Name ______________________________

Comparative and Superlative Adjectives

Directions: Write the comparative or superlative form of each adjective in ( ).

1. What is the (efficient) of all methods of producing power? ______________
2. Nuclear fusion will produce (clean) power than fission. ______________
3. Some fuels burn for a (long) time than others. ______________
4. Of all types of coal, anthracite burns the (long) time. ______________
5. Anthracite coal is one of the (hard) fuels there is. ______________
6. Bituminous coal is (soft) than anthracite coal. ______________
7. The Donets Basin is one of the (large) of all coal deposits. ______________
8. The United States has the (great) amount of coal of all. ______________
9. The (big) of all anthracite deposits is in Pennsylvania. ______________

Directions: Write the correct form of the adjective in ( ).

10. Which is the (good) region of all for coal? ______________
11. Appalachia is the (large) producer of all. ______________
12. Mining is one of the (dangerous) jobs of all. ______________
13. Liquid fuels are (convenient) than solids. ______________
14. Is oil or gas a (efficient) fuel? ______________
15. Are nuclear fuels (good) than fossil fuels? ______________
16. Someday nuclear fusion may be (common) than fission. ______________
17. Nuclear power is (economical) than coal. ______________
18. Nuclear fuels are (compact) than fossil fuels. ______________

Write a Journal Entry

On a separate sheet of paper, write a journal entry about what a day in your life would be like without electrical power. Be sure to use comparative and superlative forms of adjectives to point out differences.

Notes for Home: Your child identified comparative and superlative forms of adjectives in sentences. ***Home Activity:*** Name an adjective and have your child supply the comparative and superlative forms. Then switch roles.

Name ______________________________

REVIEW

Comparative and Superlative Adjectives

Directions: Fill in the columns below with the comparative and superlative forms of each of the adjectives given.

Adjective	**Comparative Form**	**Superlative Form**
extraordinary	**1.** ______________	**2.** ______________
hot	**3.** ______________	**4.** ______________
tame	**5.** ______________	**6.** ______________
steep	**7.** ______________	**8.** ______________
sleepy	**9.** ______________	**10.** ______________

Directions: Complete each sentence with the comparative or superlative form of the adjective in ( ). Write the adjective on the line.

______________ **11.** Mike felt as if he were the (unhappy) person in the world that day in 1935.

______________ **12.** His family's farmland had become (poor) each year, and now nothing would grow on it.

______________ **13.** He and his family were moving to a place with (rich) land—California.

______________ **14.** Mike's family was joining one of the (large) migrations, or movements, in American history.

______________ **15.** In the 1930s, over three million people in the Great Plains moved west to find a (bearable) life.

______________ **16.** Mike had packed his carving tools carefully, for nothing was (precious) to him.

______________ **17.** The figures Mike carved out of wood were some of the (beautiful) figures people had ever seen.

______________ **18.** In fact, he was (proud) of his carvings than he usually admitted.

______________ **19.** Perhaps in California, Mike could sell his figures and find a (fulfilling) life.

______________ **20.** Mike began to feel (cheerful) as the family's overloaded old car rattled west.

Notes for Home: Your child used the comparative and superlative forms of adjectives to compare people, places, and things. ***Home Activity:*** Have your child make a list of adjectives. Challenge your child to use each adjective in its comparative and superlative forms.

Name ______________________

Adverbs

An **adverb** is a word that can tell how, where, or when something happens.

Yesterday we walked quietly into the library, read the onscreen instructions for doing a title search, and eventually located a blacksmith's published diary.

Like adjectives, adverbs can be used to make comparisons. Most adverbs have three forms: the adverb itself, the **comparative** form, and the **superlative** form.

Use the comparative form when you talk about two actions. To write the comparative form of most adverbs, add the ending **-er** or the word **more.**

Gram pored over the old diary longer than Mom did.
She studied the diary entries more carefully than Mom did too.

Use the superlative form when you talk about three or more actions. To write the superlative form, add the ending **-est** or the word **most.**

Of the three of us, Gram is the one who stays longest in the Rare Books area.
She also is the one who examines those valuable books most carefully.

Most adverbs that end in **-ly** use **more** and **most** to make the comparative and the superlative forms: for example, **rapidly, more rapidly, most rapidly.**

Directions: Complete the table with the comparative and the superlative forms of each adverb.

Adverb	Comparative Form	Superlative Form
warmly	**1.**	**2.**
fast	**3.**	**4.**
quickly	**5.**	**6.**
oddly	**7.**	**8.**
soon	**9.**	**10.**
recently	**11.**	**12.**
late	**13.**	**14.**
hopefully	**15.**	**16.**
early	**17.**	**18.**
easily	**19.**	**20.**

Notes for Home: Your child learned to identify comparative and superlative forms of adverbs. ***Home Activity:*** Challenge your child to describe an activity you do together, using comparative or superlative adverbs.

Name ______________________________

Adverbs

Directions: Write the kind of adverb named in ( ) on the line to the left to complete each sentence.

______________________ **1.** Tanya waited at the blacksmith's shop. Her classmates also waited _____ . (tell where)

______________________ **2.** She had read a story _____ about blacksmiths and looked forward to seeing them demonstrate their trade. (tell when)

______________________ **3.** She _____ remembered an illustration of a blacksmith working near a hot fire. (tell how)

Directions: Write the correct form of the adverb in ( ) to complete each sentence.

______________________ **4.** "This could not have been the (easy) skill to learn," Tanya thought.

______________________ **5.** Blacksmiths have to work (hard) than many workers today.

______________________ **6.** Blacksmiths also have to work (carefully) to bend and shape the iron than workers who use machines to do this task.

______________________ **7.** A complicated design means that the blacksmith has to work (skillfully) than usual.

______________________ **8.** Tanya would probably stay (long) than her classmates.

______________________ **9.** She would watch (closely) than the other students too.

______________________ **10.** She wished the shop would open its doors (soon) than 10 A.M.!

Write a Poem

Think about a skill that you admire and a person who does that skill well. On a separate sheet of paper, write a poem about this person. Use comparative and superlative adverbs to compare this skill to another, or to compare the person's ability to another's.

Notes for Home: Your child wrote adverbs, including the comparative and superlative forms. ***Home Activity:*** Take turns making up quiz questions, using comparative and superlative adverbs. (For example, *What small boat would you have to operate most slowly?—a rowboat*)

Name ______________________________

Adverbs

Underline the adverb in each sentence.

1. I ran quickly through the park.
2. My friend ran quicker than I did.
3. Yesterday she told me she would race me to the school playground.
4. I told her I would race her today.

An **adverb** can tell how, where, or when something happens. When an adverb is used to compare two actions, the **comparative form** is used. Add **-er** or **more** to make the comparative form. When an adverb is used to compare three or more actions, the **superlative form** is used. Add **-est** or **most** to make the superlative form.

Directions: Circle the adverb in each sentence.

1. I have read this book before.
2. The story begins mysteriously.
3. I enjoyed this book more thoroughly than any other mystery book I have read.
4. The dog, Mutt, suddenly disappears.
5. He is gone faster than you can imagine.

Directions: Choose an adverb that best fits each sentence. Write it on the line to the left.

______________________ 6. The heroine Lila ________ finds Mutt.

______________________ 7. Lila ________ suspects foul play.

______________________ 8. She ________ discovers a ransom note.

______________________ 9. The kidnappers ________ demand a huge ransom.

______________________ 10. Lila gasps ________.

______________________ 11. She looks ________ for Mutt.

______________________ 12. She approaches the house ________.

______________________ 13. The kidnappers have acted ________.

______________________ 14. They ________ left open a window.

______________________ 15. Mutt arrives home ________.

Notes for Home: Your child identified and used adverbs in sentences. ***Home Activity:*** Watch a television show with your child, but turn off the sound. Have your child use adverbs in sentences to describe what the actors on the show are doing.

Name ______________________________

Adverbs

Directions: Read each sentence. Write the correct form of each adverb in ( ) on the line to the left.

________ **1.** She does her work (carefully) than you.

________ **2.** You write (neatly) of the three.

________ **3.** You write (beautifully) than I ever could.

________ **4.** Print your name (clearly) than you did last time.

________ **5.** Next time erase your mistakes (thoroughly) than this.

________ **6.** This picture is (skillfully) drawn than the first one.

________ **7.** Today our class was dismissed (early) than usual.

________ **8.** I finished (soon) of anyone.

________ **9.** I learned French (easily) than I learned German.

________ **10.** Of the whole class, who works (eagerly)?

Directions: Rewrite each sentence with the correct form of the underlined adverb.

11. Can't you run <u>more faster</u>?

____

12. Of all the bands, this one plays <u>most loudest</u>.

____

13. This building was built <u>latest</u> than that one.

____

14. These books are stacked <u>neatly</u> than those.

____

15. The movie started <u>earliest</u> than we thought.

____

16. Doesn't Venus shine <u>brightly</u> than Mars?

____

17. This car runs <u>economically</u> of all three.

____

Notes for Home: Your child wrote the correct forms of adverbs in sentences. ***Home Activity:*** Have your child create a five-box comic strip. Challenge him or her to use adverbs in captions for the comic strip.

Name ______________________________

REVIEW

Adverbs

Directions: Write the adverb that modifies the underlined verb.

______________ **1.** The world really has more than seven ancient wonders.

______________ **2.** Visitors often climb 7,000 feet to Peru's ancient city of Machu Picchu.

______________ **3.** There they see a temple and a fortress with beautiful stonework.

______________ **4.** Terraced gardens surrounded the city originally.

______________ **5.** Today visitors must imagine the city as it once looked.

Directions: Write an adverb to complete each sentence.

______________ **6.** My cousins will visit the Great Wall of China _____.

______________ **7.** They _____ will take many pictures of that amazing sight.

______________ **8.** Visitors find it hard to believe, but the wall _____ covers 4,000 miles.

______________ **9.** From the ground, one must look _____ thirty feet to see the top of the structure.

______________ **10.** The wall dates _____ to the fourth century B.C.E., but parts were later rebuilt in the fifteenth and sixteenth centuries.

Directions: Complete each sentence with the comparative or superlative form of the adverb in ( ). Write the adverb on the line.

______________ **11.** The British tour buses left London at about the same time, but our bus arrived at Stonehenge (early) of all.

______________ **12.** The question asked (frequently) was why prehistoric people built this group of stones in a circle.

______________ **13.** Certain ideas about Stonehenge are treated (seriously) than others.

______________ **14.** Scholars who claim that Stonehenge was a place of worship seem to argue (convincingly) of all.

______________ **15.** Stonehenge remains a mysterious site that affected me (deeply) than I had imagined.

Notes for Home: Your child used different kinds of adverbs to describe things that happen. ***Home Activity:*** Challenge your child to list as many adverbs as she or he can in one minute. Then have your child make up sentences with the adverbs.

Name ______________________________

Using Adjectives and Adverbs to Improve Sentences

To be vivid and precise or to be clear and interesting, a sentence needs descriptive details.

- Add adjectives to modify nouns and pronouns. They can tell which one, how many, how much, or what kind.
- Add adverbs to describe actions. They can tell when, where, and how.

Without adjectives and adverbs: The tour continued.

With adjectives and adverbs: The dull tour continued slowly.

Directions: Read each sentence. Underline each adjective and adverb. Draw an arrow to the word it modifies.

1. Komiko spoke happily about her interesting trip to Greece.
2. She travels most often to historic places.
3. In Athens, Greece, she admired the magnificent temple of Athena greatly.
4. She writes excitedly about these foreign travels.
5. On another fascinating trip, Komiko saw ancient Egyptian pyramids.

Directions: Add an adjective or adverb to make each sentence more vivid or precise. Then rewrite each sentence on the line.

6. Komiko lectures about her travels.

____

7. People await her talks.

____

8. When she gives a lecture, the hall is full.

____

9. Her slide presentations show the ruins of ancient civilizations.

____

____

10. I love to hear her talk about places.

____

Notes for Home: Your child identified adjectives and adverbs and used them to make sentences more descriptive. ***Home Activity:*** Give your child pairs of similar adjectives and adverbs, such as *quick* and *quickly*. Have him or her use each of the words in a sentence.

Name ______________________

Using Adjectives and Adverbs to Improve Sentences

Directions: Write a different adjective or adverb to replace the one that is underlined.

______________ **1.** The Great Pyramid is an impressive structure.

______________ **2.** When I was there, I listened attentively to the guide.

______________ **3.** I was curious to learn how such a structure could have been built.

______________ **4.** The Great Pyramid is one of the most famous places in Egypt.

______________ **5.** I quickly agreed to a sightseeing trip down the Nile River.

Directions: Add adjectives or adverbs to improve each sentence. Write the new sentence on the line.

6. After every trip, I return home.

____

7. Last year, I took a boat trip on the Aegean Sea.

____

8. We docked at an island called Rhodes.

____

9. I stared out at the sea.

____

10. I thought about the Colossus of Rhodes that used to tower over the harbor.

____

____

Write a Diary Entry

On a separate sheet of paper, write a diary entry about a favorite place. It can be either a place you already know or a place you'd like to visit. Use adjectives and adverbs to describe the place and the types of activities you might enjoy there.

Notes for Home: Your child identified and supplied adjectives and adverbs in sentences. ***Home Activity:*** Pick a place you and your child would like to visit. Take turns describing what you want to see and do. Use adjectives and adverbs in your sentences.

Name ______________________________

Using Adjectives and Adverbs to Improve Sentences

Circle the adjective. Underline the adverb.

1. We spoke quietly to the small child.

Add one adjective and one adverb to improve the sentence.

2. The raft floated.

____

Add **adjectives** and **adverbs** to provide more information about nouns and verbs in sentences, and to make sentences more interesting.

Directions: Add an adjective and/or an adverb to each sentence. Write the new sentence on the line.

1. The movie would begin.

____

2. My friend Janine chewed her popcorn.

____

3. The lights grew dim.

____

4. The actor appeared.

____

5. There was a conversation among the characters.

____

6. Janine laughed at parts.

____

7. People behind us asked her to laugh more quietly.

____

8. When the movie ended, we walked home.

____

Notes for Home: Your child added adjectives and adverbs to sentences to make them more interesting. ***Home Activity:*** Write some simple sentences for your child. Then have him or her add adjectives and adverbs to provide more detail for the reader.

Name ______________________________

Using Adjectives and Adverbs to Improve Sentences

Directions: Read each sentence. Underline each adjective and each adverb. Draw an arrow to the word it describes.

1. Fishing can be more exciting than some people think.
2. My grandfather tells some wild stories about frogs that ask questions clearly.
3. Sometimes he says that they generously tell him where to catch the best fish.
4. I'm not sure I believe all of his funny stories, but they make time pass more quickly.
5. Next time I go on a long trip with Grandpa, I'm going to ask him to help me create new stories.

Directions: Add adjectives or adverbs to improve each sentence. Write the new sentence on the line.

6. Boats bob in the water.

____

7. When the sun sets, you can see colors in the sky.

____

8. I like to sit on the end of our dock and watch the clouds change color.

____

____

9. My dog joins me.

____

10. I make up songs about what I see.

____

Write a Song

Write a song about what you might see when the sun goes down. Be creative. Your song may include what animals and plants do when the sun sets. Use at least two adjectives and two adverbs in your song.

Notes for Home: Your child used adjectives and adverbs to improve sentences. ***Home Activity:*** Together, listen to a favorite song. Have your child write down some of the adjectives and adverbs used in the song. Then have your child make up sentences, using those adjectives and adverbs.

Name ______________________________

REVIEW

Using Adjectives and Adverbs to Improve Sentences

Directions: Add adjectives and/or adverbs to improve the sentences below. Write each new sentence on the line.

1. A frog leaped out of the pond.

____

2. A fly landed on a leaf.

____

3. The two creatures stared at each other.

____

4. "Hello," said the frog.

____

5. "Humm," buzzed the fly.

____

Directions: Cross out any unneeded adjectives or adverbs in the sentences below. Write your new sentence on the line.

6. "Do I actually know you?" asked the friendly young green frog.

____

7. "Humm," loudly buzzed the same old fly again.

____

8. The small young frog looked at the fly thoughtfully and carefully.

____

9. Then soon he stuck out his sticky, gooey tongue, caught the fly, and immediately swallowed it instantly.

____

____

10. "Yumm," buzzed the happy, smiling frog.

____

Notes for Home: Your child improved sentences by adding needed adjectives and adverbs and removing unneeded ones. ***Home Activity:*** Have your child write some sentences about a person you both know. Then challenge your child to add and/or remove some adjectives and adverbs.

Name ______________________________

Avoiding Misplaced Modifiers

Adjectives and adverbs are called modifiers because they modify, or tell more about, nouns and verbs. In doing so, these modifiers affect the meanings of the nouns and verbs.

Phrases can affect the meaning of nouns and verbs too, as in the following sentence:

With spray paint, vandals seriously damaged the pleasant old city's appearance.

Watch for misplaced modifiers. To avoid confusion, keep modifiers close to the words they modify. Note how the meaning changes when the misplaced modifier in the sentence below is moved closer to the word it is meant to modify.

Misplaced: With nothing better to do, Judge Alvarez said that two strangers had defaced their city's buildings.

Correct: Judge Alvarez said that two strangers with nothing better to do had defaced their city's buildings.

Directions: Read each sentence. If the sentence is correct, write **C** on the line. If it contains a misplaced modifier, write **NC** on the line and circle the misplaced modifier.

__________ **1.** Foolishly, the men thought no one had seen what they had done.

__________ **2.** On the street, people had seen two men running with cans of spray paint.

__________ **3.** These witnesses called the police immediately and appeared in court later.

__________ **4.** Fortunately, the city had laws against graffiti (words and pictures drawn on walls and buildings) and owned a machine for removing it.

__________ **5.** In court, the mayor described the graffiti on one wall with an outraged face.

__________ **6.** He said that the vandals should clean the wall angrily.

__________ **7.** The guilty men faced three possible penalties: detention in jail, heavy fines, or community service.

__________ **8.** As a second chance, the judge sentenced them to community service in the city.

__________ **9.** Carefully, the relieved men agreed to operate the graffiti-removal machine.

__________ **10.** They offered to do other useful work too, and apologized sincerely for their past behavior on local TV.

Notes for Home: Your child identified misplaced modifiers. ***Home Activity:*** Say *Teri took a picture of a snake with her new camera*. Have your child identify the misplaced modifier and explain why it is misplaced (*with her new camera* seems to refer to the snake instead of to Teri).

Avoiding Misplaced Modifiers

Directions: Read each sentence. If a sentence contains a misplaced modifier, think about the word or words it should describe. Then write the sentence correctly on the line. If a sentence is already correct, write **C** on the line.

1. Mrs. Vu entered a local library full of complaints.

____

2. "The outside looks terrible," she said, "with trash, weedy grass, and no flowers."

____

3. She annoyed everyone with the same kinds of complaints.

____

4. The city needed more money to support the library badly.

____

5. Mrs. Vu suddenly stopped criticizing and started to help.

____

6. She ran fundraising auctions and found donors without much training.

____

7. Thick, green, and healthy, business people donated a new lawn.

____

8. Bright flowers pleased library users in window boxes.

____

9. As a woman of action, everyone praised Mrs. Vu's success.

____

10. Now, the librarians happily watch her daily arrival through the window.

____

Write a Project Profile

On a separate sheet of paper, write a description of a local project you would like to start or be involved with. Make sure there are no misplaced modifiers in your description.

Notes for Home: Your child identified misplaced modifiers. ***Home Activity:*** Write a sentence with a misplaced modifier such as *Sally saw the bear looking through her binoculars.* Have your child rewrite the sentence to correct the misplaced modifier.

Name ______________________________

Avoiding Misplaced Modifiers

RETEACHING

Rewrite the sentence so it makes sense.

I asked a woman if I could borrow her flashlight from down the block.

____

____

Modifiers are words or phrases that tell more about nouns and verbs. Sometimes the placement of a modifier is incorrect, and the sentence doesn't make sense. To avoid confusion, keep modifiers close to the words they modify.

Directions: Read each sentence. If the sentence is correct, write **C** on the short line. If it contains a misplaced modifier, write **NC** on the line and write the sentence correctly.

__________ **1.** A song was playing on the radio about a traveling artist.

____

__________ **2.** That girl asked me a question who was interested in painting.

____

__________ **3.** A boy in my math class offered to help me study for the test.

____

__________ **4.** My neighbor walked his dog who sings in the opera.

____

__________ **5.** The television commercial advertised a new way to brush your teeth.

____

__________ **6.** In great detail, the boy agreed to paint the castle.

____

__________ **7.** In the sky, several people saw a flock of geese flying.

____

Notes for Home: Your child identified misplaced modifiers in sentences and wrote the sentences correctly. ***Home Activity:*** Have your child use some of the sentences on this page to explain to you the importance of keeping modifiers near the words or phrases they modify.

Name ____________________

Avoiding Misplaced Modifiers

Directions: Read each sentence. If the sentence is correct, write **C** on the line. If it contains a misplaced modifier, write **NC** on the line and circle the misplaced modifier.

________ **1.** Brightly, my family saw the sun shine through the windows.

________ **2.** My brother thought it looked like a beautiful golden shower.

________ **3.** My sister needed help climbing up on the chair, who is younger than me.

________ **4.** Loudly, my grandmother told me about the foghorn that used to sound near her childhood home.

________ **5.** I whispered softly to the sleeping kitten.

Directions: Read each sentence. If a sentence contains a misplaced modifier, write the sentence correctly on the line. If the sentence is correct, write **correct** on the line.

6. A rabbit ate a carrot with long, floppy ears.

____

7. A girl trains horses in my class.

____

8. A man climbs mountains on my block.

____

9. My sister who dances is going to leave school early today.

____

10. A boy found a dog from my sister's math class.

____

Write a Funny Story

Sentences with misplaced modifiers can be funny. Write a four-sentence story with sentences that have misplaced modifiers. Then rewrite the story so that the sentences make sense. Check your work carefully to make sure you have written modifiers in the correct places.

Notes for Home: Your child identified misplaced modifiers and wrote modifiers correctly in sentences. ***Home Activity:*** Have your child read his or her funny story to you. Add a sentence with a misplaced modifier and have your child write it correctly.

Name ____

Possessive Nouns

REVIEW

Directions: Decide whether the underlined possessive noun is singular or plural. Write **S** on the line if it is singular. Write **P** if it is plural.

__________ **1.** What was the class's choice for the next field trip?

__________ **2.** The students' decision was to visit the Museum of Science.

__________ **3.** They especially wanted to see the museum's new exhibit on the Arctic.

__________ **4.** Everyone applauded as the bus's doors closed, and the class was on its way.

__________ **5.** At the museum, the students watched a short film about polar bears' habits.

__________ **6.** Animals' lives are hard in the Arctic.

__________ **7.** A seal's life is often in great danger for it is a polar bear's favorite food.

__________ **8.** People's safety cannot be guaranteed around these powerful animals either.

__________ **9.** The flapping of snowy owls' wings can be heard in parts of the Arctic.

__________ **10.** This harsh environment is also the Arctic fox's home.

Directions: Correct each underlined word by adding an apostrophe to make it possessive. Write the possessive noun on the line.

______________________ **11.** Isn't the Arctic Ocean the worlds smallest ocean?

______________________ **12.** Besss question was addressed to the museum guide.

______________________ **13.** The groups guide replied that the answer was yes.

______________________ **14.** You will not find reptiles footprints in the Arctic because these creatures cannot survive the cold.

______________________ **15.** Geeses honks can be heard, however, especially in Greenland.

______________________ **16.** Wolves howls are not unusual in the Arctic.

______________________ **17.** Parts of Canada, Russia, Iceland, and other nations are included in the Arctic, but a countrys borders are hard to find.

______________________ **18.** To many listeners surprise, the guide told the group that the Arctic Circle is not an actual place.

______________________ **19.** Rather, it is most mapmakers aid, marking the area that has at least one 24-hour day and one 24-hour night each year.

______________________ **20.** At the museum exit, childrens voices mixed with those of other visitors, who chatted about all they had learned.

Notes for Home: Your child used an apostrophe to form singular and plural possessive nouns—nouns that show ownership. ***Home Activity:*** With your child, look through a newspaper for possessive nouns. Decide which ones are singular and which ones are plural.

Name ______________________________

Pronouns

Pronouns are words that can take the place of nouns or noun phrases. Like nouns, pronouns have singular and plural forms. A singular pronoun replaces a singular noun. A plural pronoun replaces a plural noun.

Singular pronouns: I, me, you, he, she, him, her, it
Plural pronouns: we, us, you, they, them

Pronouns that show ownership are **possessive pronouns.** There are two kinds of possessive pronouns. One kind is used before nouns. The second kind stands alone without a noun following it.

Used before nouns: my, your, his, her, its, our, their
Used alone: mine, yours, his, hers, ours, theirs

Possessive pronouns, unlike possessive nouns, do not use apostrophes.

Allen has given <u>his</u> dog sled <u>its</u> first coat of yellow paint.

Directions: Choose a pronoun in ( ) to replace the underlined words in each sentence. Write the pronoun on the line.

______________________ **1.** <u>Norah, Joan, and I</u> went on a hiking trip. (We/She)

______________________ **2.** These trails were new to <u>Joan and Norah</u>. (her/them)

______________________ **3.** <u>Joan and Norah</u> felt like explorers. (We/They)

______________________ **4.** I pointed out an enormous tree to <u>Joan</u>. (it/her)

______________________ **5.** <u>The tree</u> looked as if it were hundreds of feet tall. (It/You)

Directions: Circle the correct possessive pronoun in ( ) to complete each sentence.

6. That backpack is (my/mine).

7. (My/mine) compass is in the front pocket.

8. (Their/Theirs) tent is larger than this one.

9. This tent is (our/ours).

10. (Your/Yours) sense of direction is better than mine.

Notes for Home: Your child used pronouns, such as *he, you,* and *they,* and possessive pronouns, such as *his, your,* and *theirs,* in sentences. ***Home Activity:*** Challenge your child to describe something that happened in school today, using pronouns and possessive pronouns.

Pronouns

Directions: Choose a pronoun in ( ) to replace the underlined words in each sentence. Write the pronoun on the line.

______________ **1.** The explorer talked to my friends and me. (us/them)

______________ **2.** Mr. Johnson had been to the Arctic three times. (We/He)

______________ **3.** The explorer and his colleagues are famous. (We/They)

______________ **4.** I enjoyed listening to Mr. Johnson. (him/them)

______________ **5.** My friends and I had a number of questions for Mr. Johnson. (We/They)

Directions: Choose a possessive pronoun in ( ) to complete each sentence correctly. Write the possessive pronoun on the line.

______________ **6.** The Smith family and (our/its) family have lived in Smithtown for 300 years.

______________ **7.** The Smiths' ancestors bought so much land that most of Smithtown once was (his/theirs).

______________ **8.** My great-great-grandfather claimed that 100 acres of the Smiths' land was really (mine/his).

______________ **9.** With (his/their) approval, I explored and made a list of the contents of my grandparents' attic.

______________ **10.** I told Liddy Smith that one of my family's oldest books must have belonged first to (her/my) family, not to ours.

Write a Log

Imagine that you keep a log as you travel to some faraway place, such as a polar region. On a separate sheet of paper, write several entries in your log. Describe the journey and your experiences. Tell about the people who travel with you. Use singular and plural pronouns and possessive pronouns.

Notes for Home: Your child used singular and plural pronouns, such as *he, you,* and *they,* and possessive pronouns, such as *his, your,* and *theirs*. ***Home Activity:*** With your child, describe items in your home and in your neighborhood, using possessive pronouns.

Name ______________________________

Pronouns

RETEACHING

Singular Pronouns			
I	me	my	mine
he	you	your	yours
her	she	it	him
	his	hers	its

Plural Pronouns			
we	us	our	ours
you	your	yours	
they	them	their	theirs

Complete the sentences. Write pronouns from the boxes.

1. Maria likes basketball.

__________ likes basketball.

2. Maria plays with some friends.

Maria plays with __________.

A **pronoun** takes the place of a noun or nouns. Pronouns may be singular or plural. **Possessive pronouns** show ownership.

Directions: Write the pronoun from each sentence.

1. They played basketball at Maria's house. __________

2. Maria's parents gave her a new basketball. __________

3. Maria thanked them before breakfast. __________

4. Maria is very happy with their gift. __________

5. Rachel and Tomas like it too. __________

6. Other friends will join their game. __________

7. Neighbors such as us will watch. __________

8. We should have an exciting afternoon. __________

Directions: Write a pronoun to replace the underlined word or words.

9. Maria wanted a party for her birthday. __________

10. Mr. and Mrs. Santos agreed to Maria's request. __________

11. Mr. and Mrs. Santos arranged for a surprise. __________

12. The surprise was a visit from a basketball star. __________

13. He signed a basketball for Maria and her family. __________

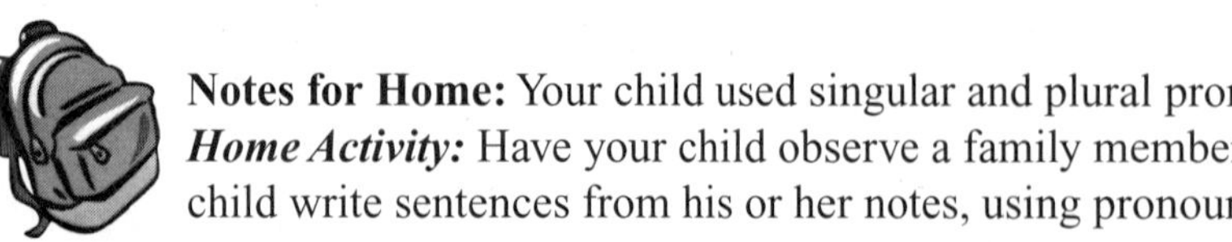

Notes for Home: Your child used singular and plural pronouns and possessive pronouns. ***Home Activity:*** Have your child observe a family member and take notes. Then have your child write sentences from his or her notes, using pronouns.

Name ______________________________

Pronouns

Directions: Circle each pronoun.

1. He built a boat and sailed it around the world.
2. She made him a flag to fly on it.
3. We sailed in my boat last week.
4. I think that her boat is bigger than ours.
5. Can you tell the difference between mine and hers?
6. Where do they store their sails?
7. Gina keeps her sails where we keep our oars.
8. Peter folds his sails and puts them aboard the boat.
9. Do you think we should take a water safety course?
10. My aunt and uncle took theirs from the Coast Guard.

Directions: Write each sentence, completing it with a pronoun that makes sense.

11. Since boating is fun, many people enjoy (pronoun) as a pastime.

____

12. Some people paddle (pronoun) own canoes.

____

13. My brother likes to fish from (pronoun) rowboat.

____

14. People with boats sail (pronoun) on breezy days.

____

15. My aunt would never sell (pronoun) motorboat.

____

16. Aunt Sal likes riding in (pronoun) so much.

____

17. (pronoun) family often rides with her.

____

Notes for Home: Your child identified pronouns in sentences and wrote sentences with pronouns. ***Home Activity:*** Together, look for pronouns in a favorite story. Have your child identify whether they are singular or plural, and whether they are possessive.

Name ______________________________

REVIEW

Pronouns

Directions: Underline the pronoun or pronouns in each sentence. Hint: Some pronouns are possessive pronouns.

1. Juan had mixed feelings about his new life in the United States.
2. The earthquake at home had caused great damage, and he and his family decided to move to America.
3. Life was good in America, but it was also strange and unfamiliar.
4. The social worker had been kind, and her advice was helpful.
5. Still, newcomers in a new land have their own particular problems.

Directions: Rewrite each pronoun and verb as a contraction.

6. we have ______________
7. he will ______________
8. she had ______________
9. they are ______________
10. it is ______________
11. I am ______________
12. we are ______________
13. you have ______________
14. they will ______________
15. you are ______________
16. we will ______________
17. he would ______________
18. she is ______________
19. I have ______________
20. he is ______________
21. it will ______________
22. you will ______________
23. she has ______________
24. he had ______________
25. they have ______________

Directions: Choose the pronoun in ( ) that completes each sentence. Write the pronoun on the line.

__________ **26.** Juan and his family were moving into (their/they're) new apartment.

__________ **27.** None of the furniture was really (their's/theirs), for they had had to leave everything behind.

__________ **28.** They thought longingly of their real home, with (it's/its) open, airy rooms.

__________ **29.** "Welcome to (your/you're) new home," said the woman who was helping them get settled.

__________ **30.** "My country is now (your's/yours)," she said.

Notes for Home: Your child identified and used pronouns—words that take the place of nouns. ***Home Activity:*** Point to different things in your home and ask questions such as "Whose is that?" Have your child respond, using a pronoun in the answer.

Subject/Object Pronouns and Agreement

A pronoun takes the place of one or more nouns or noun phrases. When a pronoun is used as the subject of a sentence, it is called a **subject pronoun.**

My family moved to a new town. We moved to a new town.

Subject Pronouns: I, you, he, she, it, we, they

A pronoun used as an object in a sentence is called an **object pronoun.** An object pronoun used as a direct object follows an action verb and tells who or what receives the action.

My dog explored the new house. My dog explored it.

Object Pronouns: me, you, him, her, it, us, them

The **referent** is the noun or noun phrase to which the pronoun refers. A pronoun and its referent must agree. A singular pronoun agrees with a singular referent. A plural pronoun agrees with one or more plural referents. A pronoun and its referent can appear in separate sentences or in the same sentence.

My parents looked for a long time. They wanted to find a good place to live.

My mother and father were sure they had made the right choice.

Directions: Write a pronoun that best replaces the underlined words in each sentence. Then write **S** if it is a subject pronoun. Write **O** if it is an object pronoun.

__________ **1.** Last April, my family moved to Acapulco, Mexico.

__________ **2.** The move surprised my brother and me.

__________ **3.** My parents said that the move would be a good experience.

__________ **4.** Later, my brother and I agreed with our parents.

__________ **5.** My brother and I enjoyed learning Spanish and living by the sea.

Directions: Underline the pronoun in each sentence. Then circle its referent.

6. When Mary first moved to Hawaii, she had a hard time making new friends.

7. Friends from home kept in touch. They called and wrote letters.

8. After a week, Mary made her first new friend.

9. Steven showed Mary the big island. He knew about many interesting places.

10. Steven and Mary biked to the top of a mountain. They could see the whole island below.

Notes for Home: Your child wrote subject pronouns and object pronouns, and identified pronouns and their referents. ***Home Activity:*** Use pronouns in sentences. Have your child tell you if each pronoun is a subject pronoun or an object pronoun.

Name ______________________________

Subject/Object Pronouns and Agreement

Directions: Write a pronoun that best replaces the underlined words. Then write **S** if it is a subject pronoun. Write **O** if it is an object pronoun.

__________ **1.** Last September, Renata arrived in town.

__________ **2.** Renata and her family came from Veracruz, Mexico.

__________ **3.** Renata taught my friends and me about Mexico and its culture.

__________ **4.** My friends and I were guests at Renata's house for a holiday called *Cinco de Mayo.*

__________ **5.** We all thanked Renata for including us in the holiday.

Directions: Underline each pronoun. Then circle its referent.

6. Ellen's family took a trip to Mexico. They saw many amazing things.

7. Ellen was interested in the Mayan ruins. She had read about the pyramids and temples.

8. Ellen first saw the Pyramid of the Sun. It was over 200 feet high.

9. When she reached the top of the pyramid, Ellen stared down at the rest of the city.

10. A guide who was with Ellen pointed out the important sites to her.

Write a Newspaper Story

On a separate sheet of paper, write a story about a current event in your town or school. Include subject and object pronouns in your composition, and make sure they agree with their referents. When you are finished, underline each pronoun and circle its referent.

Notes for Home: Your child wrote subject pronouns and object pronouns and identified pronouns and their referents. ***Home Activity:*** With your child, read a few paragraphs from a story. Have your child identify each pronoun and its referent.

Name ______________________________

Subject/Object Pronouns and Agreement

Subject Pronouns	Object Pronouns
I, you, she, he, it, we, they	me, you, her, him, it, us, them

Complete each sentence. Use a pronoun from the boxes. The clues in ( ) will help you.

1. Once ______________ (subject pronoun) wrote a message to ______________ (object pronoun).

2. ______________ (subject pronoun) looked at ______________ (object pronoun).

The **subject pronouns** are **I, you, she, he, it, we,** and **they.** A subject pronoun may be used as the subject of a sentence. The **object pronouns** are **me, you, her, him, it, us,** and **them.** An object pronoun may be used as the object in a sentence or in a prepositional phrase.

Directions: Underline each subject pronoun.

1. She knows some interesting facts about the telegraph.

2. It was the first way to send messages with electricity.

3. They could travel quickly from place to place.

4. "I want to be remembered as an inventor," Morse said.

5. "We will teach others to send messages," telegraph operators said.

Directions: Underline each object pronoun.

6. The operators taught me the code.

7. Morse's invention brought them to the world's attention.

8. People compared him to the great inventors of the past.

9. Does the telegraph affect us today?

10. The telephone, radio, and television have largely replaced it.

Notes for Home: Your child identified subject and object pronouns in sentences. ***Home Activity:*** Have your child use some of the pronouns from this page in other sentences. Ask him or her to tell you if they are subject or object pronouns.

Name ______________________________

Subject/Object Pronouns and Agreement

Directions: Write the subject pronoun from each sentence.

1. I am studying the dragonfly for science class. ____________

2. You should hear the facts about the insect. ____________

3. It has four large delicate wings. ____________

4. They look like fine netting. ____________

Directions: Write the object pronoun from each sentence.

5. The wings move them rapidly through the air. ____________

6. The speed of the insect surprised her. ____________

7. People can spot it near water in summer. ____________

8. A dragonfly's unique appearance pleases me. ____________

Directions: Write a pronoun to replace the underlined word or words in each sentence.

9. Ms. Wasp assigned a report about <u>dragonflies</u>. ____________

10. <u>The report</u> will require some research. ____________

11. <u>Pat and Toni</u> worked on theirs at the library. ____________

12. The instructor praised <u>Pam and me</u> today. ____________

13. <u>Beth</u> discovered dragonflies lay eggs in water. ____________

14. That did not surprise <u>Rafael</u> very much. ____________

15. <u>Patrick</u> said, "The adults live only a few weeks." ____________

16. <u>Kim and I</u> observed live dragonflies for hours. ____________

17. We saw <u>a dragonfly</u> eat many kinds of insects. ____________

Write an Observation Journal Entry

On a separate sheet of paper, write an observation journal entry about an insect you have seen. Use subject and object pronouns to help you explain how it looked, where it was, and what it was doing.

Notes for Home: Your child identified subject and object pronouns in sentences. ***Home Activity:*** Have your child read his or her Observation Journal Entry to you. Ask your child to underline subject pronouns and circle object pronouns.

Pronouns and Their Referents

REVIEW

Directions: In each sentence, underline the pronoun and draw a circle around its referent. Hint: Some pronouns are possessive pronouns.

1. Wanda, would you like to travel through space?
2. Spaceships were just a dream years ago, but today they are a reality.
3. Imagine how Neil Armstrong must have felt when he first stepped onto the moon in 1969.
4. Wanda would like to be the first person to step onto Mars, and perhaps she will be.
5. Many people throughout history have had their dreams about space travel.
6. This generation is the first that may see its dreams come true.
7. Astronauts in space have looked down at Earth, with its mountains and oceans.
8. Travel in outer space is exciting, but it can also be very dangerous.
9. Nevertheless, Wanda has made up her mind.
10. Look for Wanda and others someday as they zoom far out into space.

Directions: Replace with a pronoun the underlined word or words in each sentence. Write your new sentences on the lines.

11. With young people like <u>Wanda</u>, humans may actually visit other planets someday.

____

____

12. One day a spaceship may take off with <u>Wanda and other young people</u> inside it.

____

13. Years later, <u>these astronauts</u> will reach their destination planet.

____

14. When Wanda sends her first message back to Earth, what will <u>Wanda</u> say?

____

____

15. She is probably working on that first message of <u>Wanda's</u> already!

____

Notes for Home: Your child matched pronouns with their referents and rewrote sentences with pronouns. ***Home Activity:*** Work with your child to write a short dramatic scene about landing on a new planet. Have your child underline all the pronouns in the script.

Prepositions and Prepositional Phrases

A **prepositional phrase** begins with a **preposition** and ends with a noun or pronoun that is called the **object of the preposition.**

Have you seen any photos of lunar eclipses?

In the sentence above, *eclipses* is the object of the preposition *of.* Notice that the object of the preposition may have a modifier, such as *lunar.*

Common Prepositions:
about, above, across, after, along, among, around, at, before, behind, below, beside, between, by, down, for, from, in, inside, into, near, of, off, on, onto, out, outside, over, through, to, toward, under, until, up, with

Directions: Underline the prepositional phrase or phrases in each sentence. Draw a second line under the preposition. Circle the object of the preposition.

1. Astronauts in orbit have traveled around our planet.
2. In 1969, two American astronauts landed on the moon.
3. Will human visitors ever step onto the surface of Mars?
4. Our family watched TV news coverage of John Glenn's 1998 mission in space.
5. By that time, "a de-orbit burn" was part of the English language.
6. I often think about a trip across the galaxy!
7. With a telescope, I can look through the atmosphere and see into space.
8. I have read about Saturn, and it seems interesting to me.
9. The *Cassini* will reach out and study Saturn by 2004.
10. Data from *Cassini* will tell us more about Saturn's atmosphere.

Directions: Choose a preposition that makes sense in each sentence. Write the preposition on the line to the left.

__________ 11. In Roman myths, Saturn was the god _____ harvests.

__________ 12. Saturn is the sixth planet _____ the Sun, and Jupiter is the fifth planet.

__________ 13. Each of these planets travels in orbit _____ the Sun and has its own moons.

__________ 14. Saturn or Jupiter would make a good subject _____ a painting.

__________ 15. Look _____ Jupiter, huge and silvery, near an autumn moon, and dream of going there!

Notes for Home: Your child identified prepositional phrases, such as *across the galaxy.* ***Home Activity:*** Make up some short sentences. Have your child use the list of prepositions above to add prepositional phrases to each one.

Prepositions and Prepositional Phrases

Directions: Write a prepositional phrase, using the preposition in ( ). Add the phrase to the word group to form a complete sentence. Write the sentence on the line.

1. Sometimes, I imagine living (on) ______.

____

2. I would be far away (from) ______.

____

3. I would be part of a colony (of) ______.

____

4. Lighted tunnels would run (through) ______.

____

5. Fruits and vegetables would grow (inside) ______.

____

6. There might be fish (in) ______.

____

7. We would have an observatory (in) ______.

____

8. We would look at Earth (through) ______.

____

9. Fields and forests would lie (beyond) ______.

____

10. We could hide our rockets (under) ______.

____

Write a Journal Entry

Imagine that you are an astronaut. On a separate sheet of paper, write a journal entry in which you describe a day in your life on a trip to Mars. Include several sentences that use prepositions, such as *beside, into,* and *toward,* and prepositional phrases, such as *on the way* and *upon arrival.*

Notes for Home: Your child wrote prepositional phrases. ***Home Activity:*** Talk together about a trip you have taken. Have your child identify each prepositional phrase he or she uses, for example: *We traveled to the beach.*

Name ______________________

Prepositions and Prepositional Phrases

RETEACHING

Underline the prepositional phrase in each sentence.

1. Emily thinks about the colors.

2. She chooses the color of daffodils.

3. Her room looks wonderful with yellow paint.

A **preposition** relates a noun or pronoun to another word in the sentence. The noun or pronoun that follows a preposition is the **object of the preposition.** A preposition, its object, and any words that describe the object make up a **prepositional phrase.**

Directions: Underline each prepositional phrase in the sentences below.

1. Paintings called frescos are on wet plaster.

2. You can mix dry colors with egg yolks.

3. Tempera is the result of the mixture.

4. Painters once used tempera on linen surfaces.

5. Cave pictures were the earliest type of paintings.

6. Egyptians painted the walls of pharaohs' tombs.

7. Artists painted books in medieval times.

8. Small pictures appeared near letters.

9. Artists painted words and pictures by hand.

10. No printing presses existed at that time.

11. The paper consisted of long-lasting parchment.

12. We have many books made by medieval monks.

Directions: Write the prepositional phrases from the sentences above. Circle the object of each preposition.

13. ______________________

14. ______________________

15. ______________________

16. ______________________

17. ______________________

18. ______________________

19. ______________________

20. ______________________

21. ______________________

22 ______________________

23. ______________________

24. ______________________

Notes for Home: Your child identified prepositions in prepositional phrases. ***Home Activity:*** Name an animal. Have your child describe something the animal can do and use a prepositional phrase in the description. Switch roles.

Name ______________________________

Prepositions and Prepositional Phrases

Directions: Underline the prepositional phrase in each sentence. Circle each preposition.

1. We use paper in books.
2. We also use it for homework and other tasks.
3. People write letters on paper.
4. Have you ever wrapped a present in paper?
5. Some factories make paper from fibers.
6. Most paper is made with wood fibers.
7. Fibers from cloth are important too.
8. A chipping machine cuts a log into tiny chips.
9. Machines mix the chips and rags in water.
10. The mixture is treated with chemicals.
11. The watery pulp hardens between thin molds.
12. Through many machines the sheets are processed.
13. The machines press them into long paper strips.

Directions: Complete each sentence. Write prepositional phrases.

14. I use paper ______________________________.
15. I write on paper ______________________________.
16. ______________________________ I learned handwriting.
17. You can find paper ______________________________.
18. Wrapping paper is printed ______________________________.
19. Paper ______________________________ is often dull and colorless.
20. Paper comes ______________________________.
21. Many products ______________________________ are made from wood.
22. The man spoke ______________________________ at the paper factory.

Write a Description

On a separate sheet of paper, describe something you can make from paper. Use prepositional phrases in your sentences.

Notes for Home: Your child wrote prepositional phrases to complete sentences. ***Home Activity:*** Write complete subjects of sentences on slips of paper *(The baseball team)* and have your child add words including a prepositional phrase to finish the sentence. *(The baseball team cheered for each other.)*

Name ______________________

Compound and Complex Sentences

REVIEW

Directions: Write **compound** or **complex** on the line to describe each sentence.

______________ **1.** After I saw the movie *The Wizard of Oz,* I read the book.

______________ **2.** I enjoyed the movie, but I enjoyed the book even more.

______________ **3.** Who could forget Dorothy and her dog as they are blown by a tornado to the Land of Oz?

______________ **4.** Will Dorothy find her way back to Kansas, or will she have to stay in Oz?

______________ **5.** Dorothy meets a scarecrow, a tin man, and a cowardly lion, and they set off to find the Wizard of Oz.

______________ **6.** The wizard is described as all-powerful, and he may be able to grant their wishes.

______________ **7.** Scarecrow wants a brain, the tin man wants a heart, the lion wants courage, and Dorothy just wants to go home.

______________ **8.** Although the wizard turns out to be an impostor, the group's wishes do all come true.

______________ **9.** If you enjoyed *The Wizard of Oz,* you may also enjoy the many other books about Oz.

______________ **10.** L. Frank Baum must have enjoyed his own visits to the Land of Oz because he wrote more than a dozen books about it.

Directions: Use a joining word to combine each pair of sentences. Create a new sentence of the kind shown in ( ). Write your new sentence on the line.

11. You could go anywhere in the world. Where would you go? (complex)

____

12. I might want to climb Mt. Everest. I might prefer to dive deep below the ocean. (compound)

____

13. Fantastic journeys are exciting. Simpler ones can be wonderful too. (complex)

____

14. Imagine yourself on a lovely ocean beach. You will understand my point. (compound)

____

15. You travel all around the world. You will still enjoy coming home. (complex)

____

Notes for Home: Your child identified and wrote compound and complex sentences. ***Home Activity:*** Work with your child to write simple sentences about a family trip. Then use joining words to make pairs of related sentences compound or complex.

Name ______________________________

Conjunctions

Conjunctions can be used to join words, phrases, or entire sentences. Conjunctions are used to write compound subjects, compound predicates, and compound sentences. The three most commonly used conjunctions are *and, but,* and *or. And* joins related ideas. *But* joins contrasting ideas. *Or* suggests a choice between ideas.

Compound Subject: Our hearts and minds long for adventures.
Compound Predicate: We may live quietly but imagine taking trips to see marvelous things.
Compound Sentence: We may climb high mountains, or we may explore the depths of the sea.

Directions: Circle the conjunction in each sentence. Underline the two words or groups of words that the conjunction connects.

1. I went to the stage and faced my audience.
2. The men and women in the room were quiet.
3. I liked the audience but felt nervous at first.
4. I told a story about an imaginary world, and they seemed pleased.
5. Everyone in the story lived under the sea or had an island home.
6. Some people lived in hollow coral reefs, but others lived in caves beneath the sea.
7. Fish or other sea creatures were the sea dwellers' food.
8. Only a few islands and houses stood above the water.
9. The people and animals on the islands were called surface dwellers.
10. The surface dwellers never entered the sea, but no one knew why.

Directions: Use *and, but,* or *or* to complete each sentence. The words in ( ) tell what the conjunction should do. Write the conjunction on the line to the left.

______________ 11. Four-legged animals lived on the islands, _____ birds were living there too. (join related ideas)

______________ 12. Many of the birds ate berries, _____ the larger birds caught fish. (show a contrast)

______________ 13. The fisher birds ate some of the fish _____ carried the rest to the people. (add information)

______________ 14. Sea dwellers dived _____ hid among the reefs. (show a choice)

______________ 15. The sea dwellers _____ the surface dwellers remained separate societies. (add information)

Notes for Home: Your child used the conjunctions *and, but,* and *or* to complete sentences. ***Home Activity:*** Give your child two sentences with the same subject, such as *I washed the plates. I scrubbed the pots.* Have him or her use the conjunction *and* to combine the two sentences.

Name ______________________________

Conjunctions

Directions: Choose the conjunction that best completes each sentence. Write the conjunction on the line.

______________ **1.** Explorers have made long, hopeful journeys in search of treasure (but/or) a perfect society.

______________ **2.** Legends (but/and) fables have prompted some of the searches.

______________ **3.** The Spanish explorers De Niza (and/but) Coronado searched for the Seven Cities of Cibola in North America.

______________ **4.** In South America, seekers of jewels (or/but) precious metals looked for El Dorado.

______________ **5.** Even today, some groups hope to find Atlantis, an island of peace (and/but) happiness.

Directions: Use *and, or,* or *but* to combine each pair of sentences. Write the new sentence on the line.

6. Would you like to explore a whole new world? Would you rather go in search of treasure?

____

____

7. Divers can enter the underwater world. Divers can discover treasure there.

____

8. Old pirate ships lie on the ocean floor. Their chests full of coins have remained intact.

____

____

9. Cannons hundreds of years old are on those ships. Cannonballs hundreds of years old are on those ships.

____

10. Other kinds of ships also sank centuries ago. Divers are still discovering interesting objects on these old ships.

____

____

Write a Postcard

On a separate sheet of paper, write to a friend a postcard that tells about a trip to an imaginary land. Underline the conjunctions **and, but,** and **or** in your postcard message.

Notes for Home: Your child used conjunctions, such as *and, but,* and *or,* to connect ideas and form interesting sentences. ***Home Activity:*** Pick a topic and say two simple sentences related to that topic. Challenge your child to join the sentences with a conjunction.

Name ______________________________

Conjunctions

RETEACHING

A conjunction connects words, phrases, or sentences. Underline the words the conjunctions **and, or,** and **but** connect.

1. Is that insect a butterfly or moth?
2. They have pretty but delicate wings.
3. They both lay and hatch eggs.
4. Wing markings hid them easily and well.

A **conjunction** joins words or groups of words. A conjunction may join nouns, pronouns, verbs, adjectives, or adverbs.

Directions: Circle each conjunction in the sentences below.

1. Butterflies and moths are very similar.
2. Butterflies flutter and fly from plant to plant.
3. A female butterfly lays tiny but numerous eggs.
4. Larvae can see and chew.
5. They quickly grow and shed their skin often.
6. An adult life span may be only a few days or weeks.
7. Moths have feathery or smooth antennae.
8. Some species have beautiful but poisonous wings.
9. Kim and Alan gave a report about butterflies.
10. These beautiful insects fascinated them and me.

Directions: Read each sentence. Choose a conjunction that makes the most sense from those in ( ) and write it on the line.

11. Many insects (and/but) spiders spin silk threads. ______________
12. The silkworm spins the finest (and/or) strongest threads. ______________
13. Farmers handle the silkworms carefully (or/and) patiently. ______________
14. China produces more silk than Japan (or/but) South Korea. ______________
15. Show this silk scarf to her (but/and) him. ______________

Notes for Home: Your child used conjunctions in sentences. ***Home Activity:*** Say two simple sentences about something your family has done recently. Have your child use a conjunction to combine the sentences to form a compound sentence.

Name ______________________________________

Conjunctions

Directions: Circle the conjunction in each sentence. Underline the words or groups of words that the conjunction connects.

1. Andrew Jackson was a lawyer and a military leader.
2. He was orphaned and was reared by an uncle.
3. He grew to be a determined but thoughtful leader.
4. He was feared or was respected by others.
5. He brilliantly but unexpectedly won a battle.
6. You and I might enjoy a visit to his home, the Hermitage.
7. Friends and admirers supported him.
8. He campaigned hard but won easily.
9. Jackson was a courageous and clever president.
10. He supported democracy and the union of the states.

Directions: Write **and, but,** or **or** to complete each sentence below.

11. Jackson could have won ______________ lost the election.
12. He became an effective ______________ popular president.
13. Sometimes his official cabinet ______________ an unofficial "kitchen cabinet" gave him advice.
14. This group met ______________ chatted in the White House kitchen.
15. President Jackson could sign ______________ veto bills.
16. Jackson could agree ______________ disagree with a group.
17. He was a strong ______________ kindly man.
18. Young America grew ______________ prospered under his leadership.

Write a Paragraph

On a separate sheet of paper, write a paragraph about the special qualities of someone you admire. Use the conjunctions **and, but,** and **or.**

Notes for Home: Your child identified and wrote conjunctions in sentences. ***Home Activity:*** Talk with your child about the role of each conjunction in a sentence.

Name ______________________________

REVIEW

Exclamations

Directions: Decide whether each group of words is a complete exclamatory sentence. Write **S** on the line if it is a sentence. Write **N** if it is not.

__________ **1.** He really used to be a cowboy!

__________ **2.** Wow!

__________ **3.** What a piece of luck!

__________ **4.** Watch out for that horse!

__________ **5.** Be careful of those hooves!

__________ **6.** How absolutely terrifying!

__________ **7.** Just a minute, please!

__________ **8.** Whew, what a relief!

__________ **9.** I cannot imagine that!

__________ **10.** What a gorgeous horse that is!

Directions: Read each sentence. Then write an exclamation to respond to each sentence.

11. That horse just lost its shoe.

____

12. Do you think cowboys led exciting lives?

____

13. Real cowboys often had to manage thousands of cows.

____

14. Cara does not look comfortable on that horse.

____

15. What did you think of that old cowboy movie?

____

Notes for Home: Your child recognized and wrote exclamations—statements that show strong feeling and that end with exclamation marks. ***Home Activity:*** Together, write a short skit for a TV show you both know. Use some exclamations.

Name ______________________________

Interjections

Interjections are used to express strong feeling. When the feeling is especially strong, the interjection is followed by an exclamation mark. When the feeling is less strong, the interjection is followed by a comma.

Wow! That horse is wild.
Hey, get back here.

Directions: Circle the interjection in each sentence.

1. Hey! There's a cowboy movie on TV.
2. Wow! Being on a cattle drive looks like fun.
3. Ugh! It's probably harder than it seems.
4. Ouch! Falling from a horse can't feel good.
5. Hooray! They finally found that poor runaway cow.
6. Whew, that's a relief.
7. Oops, they forgot to tie up that horse.
8. Yikes! The horse is running away!
9. Oh my! He's never going to catch that horse.
10. Say, that movie was pretty good.

Directions: Choose an appropriate interjection and punctuation mark to add to the beginning of each sentence. Write the interjection on the line.

11. ______________________ Do you really own a pony of your own?
12. ______________________ I've had this pony for six months.
13. ______________________ This horse is really big.
14. ______________________ I don't know how to stop this horse!
15. ______________________ Thanks for getting him to stop.

Notes for Home: Your child identified interjections, words that express strong feeling, such as *Wow, Oh my,* and *Hey.* ***Home Activity:*** Together, write a letter or brief note to a relative. Choose a place to insert one interjection.

Name ______________________________

Interjections

Directions: Write the interjection in each sentence on the line.

______________ **1.** My, I'd like to climb a mountain like Mount Everest.

______________ **2.** Oh! Being at the top must be incredible.

______________ **3.** Say, have you ever seen films of mountain climbers?

______________ **4.** Wow! It looks like quite an adventure.

______________ **5.** Well, I think it would be very hard to do.

______________ **6.** Hey! Don't get discouraged.

______________ **7.** My goodness, they looked determined.

______________ **8.** Oh no! That cable broke.

______________ **9.** Ouch! He fell a few feet.

______________ **10.** Whew, the climber didn't get hurt.

Directions: On each line, write a sentence expressing the feeling that the interjection suggests.

11. Oh no! ______________________________

12. Good grief, ______________________________

13. Hah! ______________________________

14. What! ______________________________

15. Great! ______________________________

16. Yes, ______________________________

17. Yuck! ______________________________

18. Hey! ______________________________

19. Oops, ______________________________

20. Wow, ______________________________

Write an Advertisement

On a separate sheet of paper, write an advertisement for an adventure trip, such as rafting, mountain climbing, or going on safari. Use interjections in some of your sentences. Underline each one that you use.

Notes for Home: Your child identified interjections—words that express strong feeling—such as *Wow, Oh my,* and *Hey,* and wrote sentences using interjections. ***Home Activity:*** Challenge your child to describe something enjoyable, using interjections to show his or her feelings.

Name ______________________________

RETEACHING

Interjections

Underline each interjection.

1. Whoa! We're going so fast!

2. Eek! It's really dark in here!

An interjection is used to express strong feeling. Often an interjection is followed by an exclamation mark. If the feeling is less strong, the interjection is followed by a comma.

Directions: Circle the interjection in each sentence.

1. Aha! I've found the answer!

2. Oops, I missed that word.

3. Oh, I guess I'll go.

4. Ow! That's my sore hand.

5. Wow! I won first prize!

6. Ugh! That tastes awful.

7. Well, you finally got here.

8. Right, I understand.

9. Yikes! That scared me!

10. Whee! I love fast rides!

Directions: Write an interjection that makes sense in each sentence.

11. ____________________ We are so far away!

12. ____________________ I'm afraid of that dog.

13. ____________________ that boat is huge!

14. ____________________ I made a mistake.

15. ____________________ I guess I'd better go home.

16. ____________________ What a mess that is!

Notes for Home: Your child identified and wrote interjections in sentences. ***Home Activity:*** Together, look through old photographs. Have your child write captions for them, using interjections.

Name ______________________________

Interjections

Directions: On each line, write a sentence expressing the feeling that that interjection suggests.

1. Ugh! ______________________________
2. My, ______________________________
3. Well, ______________________________
4. Ouch! ______________________________
5. Yikes! ______________________________
6. Oh my! ______________________________
7. Say, ______________________________
8. Yes! ______________________________
9. Uh, oh! ______________________________
10. Man! ______________________________

Directions: Write on the line the interjection from each sentence.

______________ **11.** Oh no! I forgot my homework!

______________ **12.** Yuck! That milk is spoiled.

______________ **13.** Whew! That was close!

______________ **14.** Well, I guess you're right.

______________ **15.** No way! I'm not climbing that fence!

______________ **16.** Wow! I've never seen that kind of car before.

______________ **17.** Whoops, I slipped in that patch of ice.

______________ **18.** Ack! That completely slipped my mind!

______________ **19.** My, that was a long speech.

______________ **20.** All right! We won the game!

Write a Scary Story

On a separate sheet of paper, write a story about people in an imaginary scary place. Think about how characters in your story might react to different situations. Include dialogue in your story. Use interjections in some of your sentences.

Notes for Home: Your child used interjections in sentences. ***Home Activity:*** Write interjections (For example: *Wow! Oh, no! My goodness!*) on cards. Hold up a card and have your child use that interjection in a sentence.

Name ______________________________

REVIEW

Proper Nouns and Proper Adjectives

Directions: Rewrite each sentence. Capitalize each proper noun and proper adjective.

1. My brother arnold and I call our grandmother by her first name, rachel.

2. My grandfather's name is edward benedict miller, but we call him ted.

3. They live in twin falls, idaho, not too far from the snake river.

4. Recently they moved from a house on weston dr. to an apartment on ridgewood ave.

5. Rachel came to the united states from china, and ted came from great britain.

6. My family, including our irish setter, nellie, visits them every january and june.

7. Having a chinese grandmother and a british grandfather can be very interesting.

8. rachel and ted have a siamese cat and a south american parrot.

9. In their apartment building, a vietnamese neighbor lives on one side of them and an iranian family lives on the other.

10. They are really just american grandparents who live in idaho, but visiting them is like taking a trip around the world.

Notes for Home: Your child capitalized proper nouns and proper adjectives. ***Home Activity:*** Help your child write a thank-you letter, thanking someone who has helped him or her. Have your child check that all proper nouns and adjectives are capitalized.

Name ______________________________

Capitalization

Directions: When you write a letter to a friend or family member, remember to follow these rules for capitalizing words.

- Capitalize the first word of the greeting: Dear Aunt Sarah,
- Capitalize the first letter of every sentence: My grandparents came to visit.
- Capitalize the pronoun *I:* Uncle Joe and I had a lot of fun.
- Capitalize the first word of the closing: Your nephew,
- Capitalize proper nouns and proper adjectives. Remember proper nouns name particular persons, places, and things: Jana Collins, Hackensack River, American Riverboats, January 24, 2001
- Capitalize the personal titles of people: Dr. Sandra P. Weintraub

Directions: Read the following parts of a letter. Rewrite the words on the line using the correct capital letters.

1. dear Uncle joe, ______________________________
2. your friend, ______________________________
3. dear martin, ______________________________
4. sincerely yours, ______________________________
5. april 6, 2001 ______________________________

Directions: Rewrite each sentence. Use capital letters where they are needed.

6. I wanted to visit my grandparents, jacques and sophie marceau.

____

7. they used to live in amarillo, texas, but they just moved to memphis, tennessee.

____

8. Their favorite thing about Memphis is that it's next to the mississippi river.

____

9. i think their new address is 748 bishop court, but i'm not sure about that!

____

10. Their neighbors are captain dennis healy and his wife, mrs. jennifer healy.

____

Notes for Home: Your child used rules of capitalization to write different parts of a letter and to correct capitalization errors in sentences. ***Home Activity:*** Have your child write your home address using capital letters for your name, street, city, and state abbreviation.

Capitalization

Directions: Underline each word in the letter that needs a capital letter added. Then rewrite the words correctly on the lines to the right.

dear Grandpa morris,

Thank you for having me at your house last week. As i told my mom, it was one of the best visits ever. It was great fun meeting your famous neighbor, dr. Hugo p. Science. I still remember how surprised he was when we predicted that storm. If he had looked behind him at hurley's river, he would have understood. Those black clouds above the river looked like they covered all of edwards county!

your grandson,

Scott

1. ______________
2. ______________
3. ______________
4. ______________
5. ______________
6. ______________
7. ______________
8. ______________
9. ______________
10. ______________

Write a Thank-You Letter

On a separate sheet of paper, write a thank-you letter to a friend or relative. Remember to capitalize words when necessary.

Notes for Home: Your child identified and corrected capitalization errors in a letter. ***Home Activity:*** With your child, read over a letter from a friend or family member. Have your child explain why different parts of the letter are capitalized.

Name ______________________

Capitalization

RETEACHING

Capitalize the following groups of words correctly.

1. dear grandma, ______________
2. answer the phone. ______________
3. chicago tribune ______________
4. north carolina ______________
5. february 21, 2001 ______________
6. mason champlin ______________
7. 1426 wellsley dr. ______________
8. *great expectations* ______________

Capitalize all important words in a proper noun and in a title. Capitalize the first word of a greeting and a closing in a letter. Also capitalize the first word in a sentence.

Directions: Read the letter. Underline each word or group of words with a capitalization error. Write the words correctly on the lines.

2520 central st.

evanston, illinois 60201

august 13, 2001

dear uncle chris,

how are you feeling? I'm sorry you broke your leg at jones pond. I bought you a book called *fun things to do while stuck indoors.* it was written by amy sargeant. She also wrote a song called "sunny days will come again." I will sing it for you on thanksgiving. Write back soon if you feel up to it.

yours truly,

charlie

1. ______________
2. ______________
3. ______________
4. ______________
5. ______________
6. ______________
7. ______________
8. ______________
9. ______________
10. ______________
11. ______________
12. ______________
13. ______________

Notes for Home: Your child identified and corrected capitalization errors in a letter. ***Home Activity:*** Write a short letter to your child, but include some mistakes in capitalization. Have your child read the letter carefully and rewrite it correctly.

Name ______________________________

Capitalization

Directions: Answer each question with a complete sentence. Use capital letters correctly.

1. What is the name of the month in which you were born?

____

2. What is the name of your town and street?

____

3. What is the name of your favorite book, and who wrote it?

____

4. What is the name of your favorite song, and who sings it?

____

5. How would you begin a letter to a relative or close friend?

____

6. What is the name of a newspaper you have seen?

____

7. What day is it today?

____

8. What is the name of a lake or river near your town?

____

Directions: Rewrite each sentence. Use capital letters where they are needed.

9. gene has a dentist appointment with dr. grey at 8775 north bentley ave.

____

____

10. mr. fenton said the party was on saturday, june 14, 2001.

____

____

11. please buy the book *seven days in the jungle* by steven stafford.

____

____

Notes for Home: Your child used capital letters correctly in sentences. ***Home Activity:*** Have your child write a letter to a friend or relative. Help him or her check for capitalization mistakes.

Name ____________________

Compound Subjects and Objects

REVIEW

Directions: Combine each set of sentences to form a new sentence with a compound subject or a compound object. Write the new sentence on the lines. Remember to make verbs agree with their subjects and pronouns agree with their referents. (You may need to make other changes as well.)

1. Sightless people have reason to be grateful to Louis Braille. People with poor vision do too.

2. Louis Braille developed a printing system for blind people. In addition, he developed a writing system for blind people.

3. With this system of six raised dots in different combinations, people can handle reading. They can use it for writing too. They can even produce musical notation.

4. Braillewriters use keys to form letters. So do typewriters.

5. *Braille* is a type of word called an *eponym*—a word based on someone's name. *Braillewriter* is also an eponym.

Notes for Home: Your child combined sentences to form new sentences with compound subjects and compound objects. ***Home Activity:*** Together, look through books to find sentences with compound subjects and objects. Try to break each one down into two or more sentences.

Name ______________________

Commas

A **comma** is a punctuation mark that is used to set off a word or a group of words from other words. In a friendly letter, use a comma after the greeting and the closing.

Dear Louis, Sincerely, Your friend,

In a date, use a comma between the day of the week and the month, and between the day of the month and the year. In an address, use a comma between the city and the state or country.

Saturday, April 2 March 12, 1895 Gotham City, ID 06007

Commas are also used to separate three or more nouns, phrases, or clauses in a series.

The five senses are sight, hearing, smell, taste, and touch.
Some people can't see, some have no hearing, and some are unable to speak.

When you speak to, or address, a person by name or title, you are using direct address. Commas are used to set off the name when it apppears at the beginning, in the middle, or at the end of a sentence. When the name is in the middle of a sentence, two commas are used.

Thomas, is your cousin a professional dancer?
He is, Mark, and he is also deaf.
That's amazing, Thomas.

Directions: Read the following letter. Add commas where they are needed.

Dear Otto

I am reading an interesting book about people who are deaf. Did you know that some people are born deaf some become deaf from injury and others become deaf from disease? There are actors athletes and even dancers who are deaf. Dancers keep the beat by feeling the vibrations from the music.

This book has inspired me to learn sign language Otto. I'm going to write to a school for the deaf in Rochester New York. They offer to send books tapes and a videotape to help people learn sign language.

Your brother
Phillip

Notes for Home: Your child inserted commas in a letter. ***Home Activity:*** Help your child write a letter to a friend or relative. Talk about the places where commas are needed.

Name ______________________________

Commas

Directions: Read the following parts of a letter. Add commas where they are needed.

1. Your friend
2. Dear Myra
3. With love
4. November 11 1911
5. Monday February 20
6. Oakdale CA

Directions: Rewrite each sentence on the line, adding commas where they are needed.

7. Ellen did I tell you about my new invention?

____

8. It will warn me when a dog a cat or another animal enters the yard.

____

9. It works whether the animal walks runs or crawls into the yard.

____

10. The new alarm uses packing paper strings and bells.

____

11. I think you are wrong Mom when you say this system is impractical.

____

12. It will appeal to homeowners renters and landlords.

____

13. I won't charge a lot for my alarm Mom.

____

14. I'm thinking about charging two dollars three dollars or four dollars.

____

15. Did you say Mom that you would trade the alarm for a pizza tonight?

____

Write a Letter

Write a letter to someone who shares a hobby of yours, such as coin collecting, drawing, or a playing a particular computer game. Remember to use commas where necessary.

Notes for Home: Your child inserted commas in parts of a letter, in dates, in addresses, to set off a person's name, and to separate words or phrases in a series of three or more. ***Home Activity:*** Invite your child to write entries in an address book, using commas correctly.

Name ______________________________

Commas

RETEACHING

Insert commas where they are needed in each phrase or sentence.

1. Dear Jack
2. Bring me the scissors stapler and the tape.
3. I wanted to go see the new exhibit at the art museum but I didn't have time.
4. Although she looked nervous Kathy made a wonderful presentation.
5. Amanda don't you think you should be more careful with that vase?
6. We are moving to Maryland on Wednesday April 27 2001.
7. I will miss you Kari.

A **comma** is used to set off a word or a group of words from other words. In a friendly letter, use a comma after the greeting and the closing. In a date, use a comma between the day of the week and the month, and between the month and the year. In an address, use a comma between the city and the state. Use commas to separate three or more nouns or phrases in a series. Also use a comma to set off a name used in direct address.

Directions: Insert commas where they are needed in each sentence. Draw an **X** through commas that do not belong.

1. Remember, to feed the cat water the flowers and do your homework.
2. I can't do all that, in fifteen minutes Sandra!
3. I need someone to do it or I'll get in big trouble.
4. Ask Tanya. She lives at 421 Amber Road Merriwether Wisconsin.
5. I hope she is home although often she is out, on Tuesday afternoons.
6. Dina maybe you should call her, before you go.
7. I'll call her pack my things and walk there.
8. Don't forget the festival on Sunday March, 8.
9. I tried, to open the door but it was locked.
10. You need, to ring the doorbell knock on the door or try the back door.

Notes for Home: Your child inserted commas where they belong in sentences and marked commas that do not belong. ***Home Activity:*** Have your child use this page to explain to you where commas are often used.

Name ______________________________

Commas

Directions: Each sentence is missing one or more commas. Rewrite each sentence, inserting commas where they belong.

1. Yes John the correct date is October 8 1822.

____

2. I live at 42 Main Street Columbus Ohio Mrs. Gordon.

____

3. We went to London England a week later Sally.

____

4. Lee is the correct address 650 Olive Avenue Bangor Maine 04401?

____

5. By the way Heather just where is Hannibal Missouri?

____

6. Have we run out of bags or are there more back there?

____

7. This is hard work but it's for a good cause.

____

8. Doreen is a skier a pilot and a dancer.

____

9. Her patients will see Dr. Rodriguez or they will make appointments for another day.

____

____

10. Don't you think that I look terrific Louisa?

____

11. I know of a spot near 14 Olivera Street Pamplona Spain that's just like it.

____

____

12. I caught a big trout there on June 12 1998 at noon.

____

Notes for Home: Your child correctly used commas in sentences. ***Home Activity:*** Write some sentences without commas, and have your child insert commas where they belong. Help your child check his or her work.

Name ______________________________

Commas

Directions: Add a comma where needed to correct each sentence.

1. Was Euclid an ancient Greek mathematician or was he an ancient Roman?
2. Euclid lived in Greece in ancient times but we still rely on his work today.
3. Geometry students may not know Euclid's name but they learn his principles.
4. Start at one point and you can always draw a straight line to another point.
5. Measure one right angle and you will know the measurement of every other right angle.
6. Points, lines, and angles are the subjects of geometry but triangles are the subject of trigonometry.
7. Trigonometry is used to study light and electricity and it is crucial in surveying, navigation, and astronomy.
8. Euclidean geometry is basic but there are other kinds of geometry.
9. Mathematicians might work on analytic geometry or they might prefer descriptive geometry.
10. Much has been learned since Euclid's day but his work remains the starting point.

Directions: Add a comma where needed to correct each sentence. If no comma needs to be added, write **N** on the line.

__________ **11.** If you could meet someone from the past would you like to meet Euclid?

__________ **12.** Although he was a brilliant mathematican, he may not have been fun to talk to, one-on-one.

__________ **13.** While you are meeting mathematicians, you might want to talk to Descartes.

__________ **14.** Descartes worked on geometry after Euclid had been dead for centuries.

__________ **15.** Although Euclid lived so long ago his principles are still used and tested hundreds of years later.

__________ **16.** Amazingly, Euclid's principles are still recalled by mathematicians whenever they use geometry.

__________ **17.** "If you want to find the area of a rectangle" explained Mr. Sams, "multiply the length of the base by the height."

__________ **18.** If you do not multiply the base by the height and divide by 2 you will not find the area of a triangle.

__________ **19.** After you use such calculations a few times you will find them less difficult.

__________ **20.** "When you study geometry" Mr. Sams said, "remember to think of Euclid and thank him."

Notes for Home: Your child added commas where needed to punctuate compound and complex sentences correctly. ***Home Activity:*** Read aloud an interesting written passage for your child to write down. Then help your child check that commas were used correctly.

Name ______________________________

Quotation Marks and Paragraph Indentation

A **direct quotation** is made up of the exact words a speaker says. When you write a direct quotation, enclose it in quotation marks (" "), and capitalize the first word. Begin a new paragraph each time the speaker changes.

Use commas to set off words that introduce a direct quotation. Place the comma that ends the quotation inside the quotation marks. If the quotation is a question or exclamation, place the question or exclamation mark inside the quotation marks.

Ms. Fisher said, "Today, you will do an experiment."
"What will we do today?" Jolene asked.

In interrupted quotations, a comma is used when the second part of the quotation does not begin a new sentence. If the second part begins a new sentence, a capital letter and proper end mark are used in this second part.

"What," asked Robert, "will the experiment be about?"
The class waited in silence.
"We will observe acceleration," Ms. Fisher said. "You will use marbles of different sizes, a ramp, and a stopwatch."

Directions: Use quotation marks to enclose the direct quotation in each sentence.

1. I want to see what it's like to live without clocks, Ken said.
2. Sarah said, What do you mean?
3. What I mean, Ken said, is that I want to test my sense of time.
4. If I take a walk, Ken said, will I be able to guess how long I have been walking?
5. Or will you be able to tell about what time of the day it is? Sarah said.
6. Right, now you understand, Ken said.
7. I'd like to know whether I would do things faster or more slowly, if I wasn't looking at a clock, said Jenny.
8. That's a good idea, Sarah said. Let's try it.
9. I'll carry a watch, Lori said, but none of you will look at it.
10. I'll list the times, Lori continued, at which we start and finish things.

Notes for Home: Your child inserted quotation marks before and after direct quotations. ***Home Activity:*** With your child, write a few sentences of a conversation. Have your child insert quotation marks before and after the exact words each person says.

Name ______________________________

Quotation Marks and Paragraph Indentation

Directions: Add quotation marks, commas, end marks, and capital letters to form complete sentences. Write the sentences on the lines.

1. please do your geometry homework now Mom said

____

2. what makes you think that I'm not going to do it I asked

____

3. I know you like to put off your homework Mom replied.

____

4. Then she added but geometry is very important

____

5. what do you mean by that I asked

____

6. without geometry Mom answered life itself would be impossible

____

7. mom I answered i think that's a little extreme

____

8. she replied maybe I am speaking a little too strongly

____

9. I know why I said

____

10. you can't help it I added you're my geometry teacher

____

Write a Conversation

On a separate sheet of paper, write a few lines of a conversation between two characters. Have them work out a complicated math problem. Remember to use quotation marks and punctuate each sentence correctly. Start a new paragraph each time the speaker changes.

Notes for Home: Your child used quotation marks and other punctuation marks to set off direct quotations. ***Home Activity:*** With your child, listen to a conversation on a television show. Have your child "insert quotation marks" before and after each person's words, using hand gestures.

Name ______________________________

Quotation Marks and Paragraph Indentation

Study the following quotations. Then insert quotation marks, commas, periods, question marks, and exclamation marks where they belong.

I have a question he said

She replied Go ahead

Why does an elephant have wrinkles he asked

It's hard to iron an elephant she answered

That he sighed is not very funny

You're wrong she laughed It's hilarious

Use **quotation marks** to show the exact works of a speaker.

Directions: Write each quotation using capital letters and punctuation correctly.

1. I threw the clock so I could see time fly said Dotty.

____

2. Meet me at the corner said the wall to the ceiling

____

3. The elevator sighed life has its ups and downs

____

4. How do you know it is raining cats and dogs asked Fern

____

5. Because I just stepped in a poodle exclaimed LaVerne.

____

6. Which hand do you write with Willy inquired

____

7. I do not write with my hand said Nilly I write with a pencil

____

Notes for Home: Your child punctuated quotations. ***Home Activity:*** Let your child listen to a conversation between you and another family member. Have your child write part of the conversation, using quotation marks to signal a speaker's exact words.

Name ____________________

Quotation Marks and Paragraph Indentation

Directions: Add all necessary punctuation to the sentences below.

1. Pyramids are interesting structures said Marie
2. Philip asked Who built them
3. Egyptians built many of them replied Marie
4. In the Americas added Mrs. Conti the Mayans built pyramids
5. Egyptian pyramids are very old remarked Marie
6. You are right noted Mrs. Conti They were built from about 2700 B.C. to about 1000 B.C., thousands of years ago
7. Why were they built asked Philip
8. Marie explained Egyptian pyramids were used as tombs for royalty

Directions: Rewrite the conversation below. Use correct punctuation and capitalization. Begin a new paragraph each time the speaker changes.

9.–17.

the largest pyramid in Egypt Marie remarked is the Great Pyramid. I read about it in the encyclopedia said Jeff it is amazing. it is one of the Seven Wonders of the World explained Mrs. Conti. how big is it asked Philip. It is nearly five hundred feet tall said Jeff. each side measures over seven hundred fifty feet added Marie. wow exclaimed Philip it must have contained some treasure. you can see it continued Marie if you travel to Egypt.

Notes for Home: Your child correctly wrote and punctuated a conversation. ***Home Activity:*** Have your child write an imaginary conversation between two made-up characters. Help him or her add quotation marks to signal a speaker's exact words.

Name ______________________

REVIEW

Quotation Marks

Directions: Rewrite the sentences, adding capital letters, quotation marks, commas, periods, question marks, and exclamation marks as needed.

1. are you trying out for the band asked Jerome

____

2. i'd like to said Lydia but I'm not sure I'm good enough

____

3. that's silly exclaimed Jerome you're a good clarinet player

____

4. Lydia smiled and said do you really think so

____

5. Yes, I think so replied Jerome and the band leader will think so too

____

Directions: Write a sentence that uses each group of words as a quotation.

6. you can start playing now, Lydia

____

____

7. thank you. that was very good

____

____

8. do you think I passed the audition

____

____

9. well, Lydia, welcome to the band

____

____

10. great I did it

____

____

Notes for Home: Your child corrected and wrote sentences that included quotations. ***Home Activity:*** Have a conversation with your child about a favorite song or musical group. Then challenge your child to write the conversation as if it were part of a story.

Name ______________________________

Contractions

A **contraction** can be formed by combining a pronoun and a verb. An apostrophe replaces the letter or letters that are left out. Here are some common contractions:

Pronoun + Verb	Contraction	Pronoun + Verb	Contraction
I am	I'm	I will	I'll
she is	she's	he has	he's
it is	it's	it has	it's
you are	you're	we have	we've
they are	they're	I would	I'd

Contractions can also be formed by combining a verb and *not*. Since *not* is a negative word, these contractions are called **negative contractions.** Here are some common negative contractions.

Verb + *not*	Negative Contraction	Verb + *not*	Negative Contraction
are not	aren't	do not	don't
is not	isn't	does not	doesn't
were not	weren't	did not	didn't
was not	wasn't	has not	hasn't
would not	wouldn't	have not	haven't

Use only one negative to make a sentence mean "no" or "not."
Don't write: Don't never do that again.
Write: Don't do that again.
Or: Never do that again.

Directions: Combine each pair of words to form a contraction. Write the contraction on the line.

1. he will ____________________
2. would not ____________________
3. she has ____________________
4. does not ____________________
5. they are ____________________
6. I have ____________________

Directions: Combine each pair of words in ( ) to form a contraction that completes each sentence. Write the contraction on the line.

____________________ 7. (I would) like to learn how to play the guitar.

____________________ 8. (It is) an instrument that you can play alone.

____________________ 9. (You have) listened to guitar players, haven't you?

____________________ 10. I (have not) heard any sound quite as beautiful.

Notes for Home: Your child practiced writing contractions. ***Home Activity:*** Play a matching game. Write words such as *I am, he has,* and *are not* on index cards. Then write the contraction for each on another set of cards. Place them face down and try to pick a matching pair.

Name ____________________

Contractions

Directions: Match each word in the column to the left with its contraction in the column to the right. Write the letter of the matching contraction on the line.

________	**1.** they have	**a.** he's
________	**2.** is not	**b.** you're
________	**3.** he has	**c.** I'd
________	**4.** we will	**d.** we'll
________	**5.** you are	**e.** isn't
________	**6.** were not	**f.** doesn't
________	**7.** it is	**g.** it's
________	**8.** I had	**h.** they've
________	**9.** you have	**i.** you've
________	**10.** does not	**j.** weren't

Directions: Choose a contraction from the box to complete each sentence. Write the contraction on the line to the left.

she's	we'd	aren't	she'd	isn't

________________ **11.** For Kelly, there _____ anything more fun than painting.

________________ **12.** _____ do it every day if she had time.

________________ **13.** Kelly says that there _____ enough hours in the day to do everything she wants to do.

________________ **14.** I think Kelly is a great musician, but _____ not so sure of herself.

________________ **15.** My friends and I told her that _____ all come to her concert.

Write a Journal Entry

On a separate sheet of paper, write a journal entry about a song that you really like. Tell what the song means to you. Include some contractions.

Notes for Home: Your child practiced writing contractions, such as *aren't* for *are not*. ***Home Activity:*** Say some sentences, using a few of the contractions on this page. Encourage your child to tell you the two words that form each contraction.

Name ______________________________

Contractions

RETEACHING

Write the contraction for each pair of words.

1. I have ____________ **2.** she has ____________ **3.** they will ____________

4. you are ____________ **5.** is not ____________ **6.** would not ____________

A **contraction** is a short way to write two words. It is formed by taking out one or more letters and replacing them with an apostrophe **(')**. A contraction can be formed by combining a pronoun and a verb or by combining a verb and the word *not.*

Directions: Circle the correctly spelled contraction for each pair of words at the left.

1. will not	willn't	won't	will'not
2. can not	can't	cant	cann't
3. she had	shed'	shed	she'd
4. should not	shouldnt	shouldn't	should'nt
5. have not	haven't	have'nt	havent
6. we are	were	we're	wer'e
7. she will	she'll	shell	shel'l
8. do not	don't	do'nt	dont
9. you had	youd	yo'ud	you'd
10. he is	hes	he's	he'was
11. were not	were'nt	weren't	werent'
12. I will	Ill	I'wll	I'll
13. had not	had'not	hadt'	hadn't
14. there is	there's	theres	ther'is
15. was not	was'not	wasn't	wa'nt

Notes for Home: Your child identified contractions that were spelled and punctuated correctly. ***Home Activity:*** Have your child use some of the contractions on this page in sentences. Ask your child to form contractions of other word pairs, such as *might have* or *you have.*

Name ______________________

Contractions

Directions: Form twenty contractions by choosing one word from each box and writing the contraction on the line.

I	can	might
she	have	were
he	has	was
we	did	you
they	do	

am	not
are	will
was	have
were	has
is	had

1. ______________ 2. ______________

3. ______________ 4. ______________

5. ______________ 6. ______________

7. ______________ 8. ______________

9. ______________ 10. ______________

11. ______________ 12. ______________

13. ______________ 14. ______________

15. ______________ 16. ______________

17. ______________ 18. ______________

19. ______________ 20. ______________

Directions: Choose a contraction from the box that best completes each sentence. Write the contraction on the line to the left.

you've	don't	haven't	hasn't	shouldn't

______________ **21.** I _________ been able to read for pleasure since we moved far away from the library.

______________ **22.** As long as _________ got a library card, you will always have something to read.

______________ **23.** Please _________ walk on the flowers.

______________ **24.** I know it is important to you, but you _________ leave school to go to the concert.

______________ **25.** She _________ visited Grandma in three months.

Write a Poem

On a separate sheet of paper, write a poem about what you can do and what you would like to be able to do better. Use contractions in your poem.

Notes for Home: Your child formed contractions and used contractions in sentences. ***Home Activity:*** Together, watch ten minutes of a television program. Have your child write as many contractions as possible that were used in the program.

Name ____

REVIEW

Conjunctions

Directions: Use the conjunctions *and, but,* and *or* to complete the sentences. Write the conjunction on the line to the left.

__________ **1.** You may think you want to be an architect, _____ you should consider these questions first.

__________ **2.** Do engineering _____ art both appeal to you?

__________ **3.** When you travel, would you rather look at buildings _____ go to the beach?

__________ **4.** Architects may enjoy the beach, _____ buildings come first.

__________ **5.** If you enjoy building things _____ drawing pictures, perhaps architecture is the career for you.

Directions: Combine each pair of sentences with the conjunction *and, but,* or *or.*

6. *Form* refers to the appearance of a building. *Function* refers to its purpose.

____

____

7. Does form depend on function? Does function depend on form?

____

____

8. Architects are always asking this question. No one has found the final answer.

____

____

9. Is beauty more important? Is comfort more important?

____

____

10. Architects may not agree on the answer. They still manage to design wonderful buildings.

____

____

Notes for Home: Your child used the conjunctions *and, but,* and *or* to complete and combine sentences. ***Home Activity:*** Make a card for each of the three conjunctions. Then make word cards. Take turns choosing two word cards and a conjunction card to use in forming a sentence.

Name ______________________________

Semicolons, Colons, and Hyphens

Semicolon (;)

- Use a semicolon to join two closely related, short sentences:
  Friends and neighbors worked hard; the barn was built in a day.

Colon (:)

- Use a colon to separate the hour from the minute: 8:45 P.M.
- Use a colon to punctuate the greeting in a business letter: Dear Senator Young:
- Use a colon to introduce a list that comes after words like *following* or *these:*
  These are some of the creative arts: painting, sculpture, and architecture.
- Use a colon to set off the name of a speaker in a play:
  MOLLY: I've never told anyone this, but I want to be an architect someday.

Hyphen (-)

- Use a hyphen to join words that are thought of as one:
  Michelangelo was a well-known sculptor, painter, and architect.
- Use a hyphen to write the numbers twenty-one to ninety-nine.

Directions: Join each pair of sentences with a semicolon. Write the new sentence on the line.

1. I like to stand and stare at buildings. Someday I think I'll try to design one.

____

____

2. Some architects specialize in skyscrapers. Other architects specialize in bridges or tunnels.

____

____

Directions: Add a colon or a hyphen to each sentence.

3. The reasons I want to design buildings are these they last a long time, they're useful and necessary, and they can be very beautiful.
4. I may be soft spoken, but I work very hard to get what I want.
5. My first architecture class begins at 9 30 A.M.

Notes for Home: Your child used semicolons (;), colons (:), and hyphens (-). ***Home Activity:*** Have your child explain four different ways to use colons.

Name ______________________

Semicolons, Colons, and Hyphens

Directions: Use a semicolon to join a sentence in the first column to a sentence in the second column. Write each new sentence on the matching numbered line.

1. I want to travel.	**a.** Every year it tilts a little bit more.
2. I especially love modern skyscrapers.	**b.** My favorite is the Sears Tower in Chicago.
3. I want to see the Leaning Tower of Pisa.	**c.** They were built five thousand years ago.
4. I also want to go to Egypt to see the pyramids.	**d.** That way, I can see the great buildings of the world.

1. ______________________

2. ______________________

3. ______________________

4. ______________________

____

Directions: Add a colon and a series of items to complete each sentence.

5. To build these bird houses, we need the following materials ______________________

____

6. These are the birds we want to attract ______________________

____

7. Good teamwork requires the following skills ______________________

____

Directions: Use a hyphen to combine the two words given. Write the new word on the line.

8. well, liked ______________________

9. eighty, nine ______________________

10. vice, president ______________________

Write a Description

On a separate sheet of paper, write a description of the most beautiful building you've ever seen. Tell what you know about the building's history, including when it was built and how it's been used. Include colons, semicolons, and hyphens as needed in your description.

Notes for Home: Your child used semicolons (;), colons (:), and hyphens (-). ***Home Activity:*** Write two sentences that can be combined with a semicolon, such as *I like plays. However, I like movies better*. Have your child use a semicolon to combine the two sentences.

Name ______________________________

Semicolons, Colons, and Hyphens

RETEACHING

Insert a semicolon to join the pair of sentences. Write the new sentence.

1. My brother and I love reading. However, we haven't had time to go to the library this week.
2. ____

____

Insert colons where they belong.

3. Please bring the following shoes, socks, and a bucket.
4. I arrived at 4 30.
5. Dear Governor Smith
6. GENE Look out!

Insert hyphens where they belong.

7. She had a worn out hat.
8. Read page fifty eight.

Semicolons are used to join two short sentences that are closely related. **Colons** are used to separate the hour from the minute when giving the time. Colons are also used to punctuate the greeting in a business letter, to set off the name of a speaker in a play, and to introduce a list. **Hyphens** are used to join words that are thought of as one word, and to write the numbers twenty-one to ninety-nine.

Directions: In each sentence, add a colon or a hyphen where it belongs.

1. She had these three ideas for a project making a collage, building a model, and painting a portrait.
2. Mr. Nevins looks young, but he is sixty two.
3. BARBARA I wonder where they are.
4. Dear Doctor Fields

Directions: Join the pair of sentences with a semicolon. Write the new sentence on the line.

5. Our friends were avid skiers. Colorado was their home away from home.

____

____

Notes for Home: Your child used colons, semicolons, and hyphens to correctly punctuate sentences. ***Home Activity:*** Have your child find in a newspaper or magazine examples where colons, semicolons, and hyphens are used. Ask your child to explain the punctuation in one example.

Name ______________________________

Semicolons, Colons, and Hyphens

Directions: Insert colons, semicolons, and hyphens where they belong.

THE TRICKY BEAR

These are the characters Lucy, Bud, and a Bear. The play starts at 5 00 in the afternoon.

BUD We're lost. What do we do now?

LUCY Bud, don't be so negative. This is a very pleasant grove of trees.

BUD Hey, what's that?

LUCY Looks like a falcon. *(rubbing her hands together)* Just look at those gleaming talons.

BUD It's quite obvious you're trying to scare me however, it won't work. *(A fierce growl is heard offstage.)* Yikes! It's a bear!

LUCY Don't be silly. It's probably one of the other kids trying to trick us.

BUD A lot you know. I'm getting out of here. *(He hesitates.)* Wait. What if I run right into it?

LUCY Climb that tree. But there aren't any bears within eighty nine miles of here.

BUD That's no good—bears can climb trees. *(The growling sound is very loud now.)* I'm getting out of here!

(Bud runs off just as the bear runs in, and they collide. As they fall, the Bear's head comes off and we see that it is Kevin, a friend of theirs.)

Write an Ending

On the lines, write an ending to the script you corrected. Think about what the characters might say to each other, and how they might act. Use colons where they belong. Also use at least one semicolon and one hyphen.

BUD ____

____

KEVIN ____

____

LUCY ____

____

Notes for Home: Your child correctly used colons, semicolons, and hyphens to punctuate a script for a play. ***Home Activity:*** Together, write a short script of a conversation during a family meal. Help your child punctuate the script correctly.